PORTRAITS
OF
AMERICAN PHILOSOPHY

PORTRAITS
OF
AMERICAN PHILOSOPHY

Edited by Steven M. Cahn

ROWMAN & LITTLEFIELD
Lanham • Boulder • New York • Toronto • Plymouth, UK

Published by Rowman & Littlefield
4501 Forbes Boulevard, Suite 200, Lanham, Maryland 20706
www.rowman.com

10 Thornbury Road, Plymouth PL6 7PP, United Kingdom

British Library Cataloguing in Publication Information Available

Library of Congress Cataloging-in-Publication Data

Portraits of American philosophy / edited by Steven M. Cahn.
pages cm
Includes bibliographical references and index.
ISBN 978-1-4422-2333-2 (cloth : alk. paper) -- ISBN 978-1-4422-2334-9 (electronic)
1. Philosophy, American--20th century--Biography. I. Cahn, Steven M.
B935.P665 2013
191--dc23
2013012114

∞™ The paper used in this publication meets the minimum requirements of
American National Standard for Information Sciences Permanence of Paper
for Printed Library Materials, ANSI/NISO Z39.48-1992.

Printed in the United States of America

In memory of

Sidney Hook (1902–1989)

and

Ernest Nagel (1901–1985),

past presidents of the Eastern Division of
the American Philosophical Association,

past officers of The John Dewey Foundation,

each other's dearest friend,

and my inspiration.

CONTENTS

Acknowledgments   ix

Introduction   I
  Steven M. Cahn

I A Life in Philosophy   5
  Nicholas Wolterstorff

2 Sixty Years of Philosophy in a Life   25
  J. B. Schneewind

3 How It Was   47
  Judith Jarvis Thomson

4 A Philosopher's Calling   63
  Ruth Barcan Marcus

5 The Romance of Philosophy   87
  Richard J. Bernstein

6 Reflections of My Career in Philosophy   105
  Harry Frankfurt

7 God and Evil among the Philosophers   129
  Marilyn McCord Adams

8 Unnatural Lotteries and Diversity in Philosophy   151
  Claudia Card

Index   I7I

About the Contributors   I8I

ACKNOWLEDGMENTS

I am most grateful to the distinguished philosophers who delivered John Dewey Lectures and reviewed them for this volume.

I also wish to express my appreciation to Jon Sisk, my long-time editor, for his advice and encouragement; to his assistant, Benjamin Verdi, for his support; to Marissa Parks for her initial advocacy; to senior production editor Alden Perkins for her thoughtful assistance, and to other members of the staff at Rowman & Littlefield for valuable help.

Please note that these lectures are published with the permission of the John Dewey Foundation. The appendix to the lecture by Ruth Barcan Marcus is used with the permission of Judith Jarvis Thomson. All John Dewey Lectures may be found in the *Proceedings and Addresses of the American Philosophical Association*.

INTRODUCTION

Steven M. Cahn

Beginning in December 1964, and each subsequent year for decades after, I attended the Eastern Division Meetings of the American Philosophical Association. During that period, I also occasionally traveled in the spring to the Central or Pacific Division Meetings. While participants at these gatherings focused on listening to lectures, interviewing candidates for faculty positions, and networking with colleagues and publishers, little opportunity was presented to reflect on the personal side of academic life: kindnesses offered, disappointments suffered, discord endured, dreams fulfilled.

Amid the whirl of convention activity, the only moment when such emotion regularly came to the fore occurred in the business meeting, where the presiding officer read the names of those philosophers who had died during the preceding year. While a few were well known, most were not, but as the list was recited, a shadow seemed to pass over the room, as the small assemblage, standing for a moment of silence, reflected perhaps on an unknown time in the future when their own deaths would be reported in this very setting. After a few moments, though, the audience retook its seats, and any hint of melancholy disappeared.

I, however, always wondered about the lives of those late scholars. How had their careers unfolded? Who had spurred their interests? Who had aided their academic efforts?

At most conferences, such questions do not occupy anyone's attention. Indeed, retired professors are rarely at the center of activity; many do not even make an appearance. Their names may still be known, but their faces are no longer recognized.

To help remedy this situation, several years ago, in my role as president of the John Dewey Founation, I proposed to the other members of the Board, Professors Karen Hanson of the University of Minnesota, Israel Scheffler of Harvard University, and Robert Westbrook of the University of Rochester, that each year we sponsor lectures at the three annual meetings of the American Philosophical Association, inviting distinguished senior scholars, chosen by the Divisional Executive Committees, to reflect on how their careers had been influenced by the people and issues of their times.

My colleagues strongly supported the idea, and we named the lectures in honor of John Dewey, widely regarded as the leading American philosopher of the first half of the twentieth century. Born in 1859 in Burlington, Vermont, where he attended elementary and secondary schools and was graduated from the University of Vermont, he held appointments at the University of Michigan, the University of Minnesota, the University of Chicago, and finally at Columbia University, where he taught for decades. The author of forty books and more than seven hundred articles, he made major contributions to virtually every area of philosophy. In addition to lecturing worldwide, he played a key role in political debates of his time, and was a founder of the American Association of University Professors, the American Civil Liberties Union, and the New School for Social Research. To celebrate his eightieth birthday, the American Philosophical Association named him its honorary president and requested that he retain this title for the duration of his life, the only person ever so recognized. Dewey died in 1952, his political awareness having experienced the development of the United States from the end of the Civil War to the tumultuous years of the Truman administration. Linking him, therefore, to these lectures about the development of American philosophy and philosophers seemed fitting.

All three divisions agreed to participate, and the first lecture was given in 2006. Not all the speakers have focused on how their early years and later successes were affected by the individuals and trends on the American philosophical scene, but some lecturers have offered rich and compelling accounts of these matters. In any case, today the presentation of the John Dewey Lecture has become a highlight at each national meeting of the American Philosophical Association.

Publishing constraints required a difficult choice from among the twenty addresses delivered thus far. Those I selected were all by past presidents of the American Philosophical Association or related scholarly societies and remind us that the life of a scholar is not only an adventure in ideas but also a tale of personal struggle.

In these talks (reprinted here in virtually their entirety), we find insightful accounts of major themes in American philosophy since 1950. These include the temporary dominance of logical positivism and then ordinary language philosophy; the animus between some supporters of so-called analytic philosophy and Continental philosophy; barriers built on prejudice of religion, race, gender, and sexual orientation; the impact of the Civil Rights movement, the Vietnam War, and feminism; new approaches to research in a variety of sub-fields; and deepened understanding of how the history of philosophy can be enriched through concentrated textual and contextual study. Also included are profiles of leading philosophy departments of the time, including those at Harvard, Princeton, Columbia, Yale, and Cornell, as well as a detailed account of the rise and decline of the remarkable philosophy program developed at the Rockefeller Institute (now Rockefeller University).

Here we find stories about a host of influential figures who played significant roles in post–World War II American philosophy. Some of their names are no longer as familiar as they once were, but their contributions deserve to be recalled and appreciated. Such is what our authors have done in these revelatory and touching reminiscences.

I

A LIFE IN PHILOSOPHY

Nicholas Wolterstorff

I

I was a graduate student at Harvard from 1953 to 1956. Let me draw a picture of what it was like to be a graduate student in philosophy then and there. To everybody under fifty in this room, it will seem a strange and alien bygone era.

There were, as I recall, twenty-one of us who were admitted as first-year grad students in philosophy that year. All of us were Caucasian: to the best of my memory, there was just one woman. A good deal of camaraderie developed among us over the course of the year. A requirement of the program was that one take written prelims at the end of the first year, four in two days. The results were posted about a week after the exams were concluded. Four of us were allowed to continue to the PhD: Clem Dore, Tom Patton, Bob Wolff, and myself. The rest were sent packing, a few with master's degrees, most without. It was hard to celebrate.

Carl Hempel taught us symbolic logic; he was visiting for the year from Princeton while Quine was spending a year at Oxford. Not a word was said about modal logic. Remember, this was before Kripke wrote his seminal paper. C. I. Lewis, one of the Harvard greats, then retired, had developed modal logic. But the regnant attitude, as I remember it, was that modal logic was fine as a game for logicians to play but of no importance for philosophers. When Quine returned the following year,

he taught a course on "word and object" that I took or audited, I forget
which; this became the substance of his book by that title.

I took a course on metaphysics from D. C. Williams. Williams was a
superb teacher, a fine philosopher, very witty, and not one to run with
the crowd. Metaphysics became my first love; I did my dissertation
under Williams's direction. And let me here pay tribute to another
student of Williams, David Lewis, probably the most gifted philosopher
of my generation. Roderick Firth taught the introductory course in
epistemology. Harvard had just chosen him over Roderick Chisholm to
fill their position in epistemology. I found the course a crashing bore;
Firth wasn't boring, the subject was boring. Only in retrospect do I
understand why that was. Meta-epistemology had not yet arisen; something in the region of classical foundationalism was simply taken for
granted as the truth of the matter, no questions asked. The course dealt
with puzzles and problems generated by this epistemology. We spent
quite some time worrying about the so-called problem of the speckled
hen; I no longer remember what that problem was. One day Firth
wanted to discuss the problem raised by double images, so he asked all
of us to press our eyeballs so that we would have some double images
right there in class. Speckled hens had been left to our imagination. I
did as I was told, but got no double images. I kept my failure to myself,
out of fear of being ridiculed by my classmates for either having a
malformed eyeball or not being able to perform so elementary an operation as pressing my eyeball to get double images.

Though meta-epistemology was nonexistent, metaethics was all the
rage. Or rather, a very narrow species of metaethics was all the rage.
The talk was all about the language of ethics. Charles Stevenson was
visiting one year and dwelt, naturally, on emotive theories of ethical
language. R. M. Hare's book on *The Language of Morals* had just appeared; the Harvard philosophers seemed not yet to know how to deal
with it.

There was no course in political philosophy—none that caught my
attention, anyway. Rawls arrived in the fall of the year I left. Henry
David Aiken taught a course in aesthetics; I stayed away from it because, from what I heard, it seemed little more than armchair psychologizing. The word "hermeneutics" was never mentioned; we interpreted
texts but never talked about interpretation of texts. There was no course
in philosophy of religion; the only glimmer I got that there might be

such a subject was the collection *New Essays in Philosophical Theology*, published in 1955 by Flew and Macintyre. I read the essays shortly after the collection appeared; I remember being struck by how worried the writers seemed. Can we even talk about God?

When it came to history, we leaped straight from Aristotle to Descartes, the assumption being that nothing of interest to present-day philosophers occurred in antiquity after Aristotle or in the Middle Ages. Aiken taught a course in the British empiricists. By the time we were about two-thirds of the way through book 2 of Locke's *Essay*, everybody, including Aiken, was bored with Locke's plodding talk about ideas, so we simply skipped the great book 3 of the *Essay* and the even greater book 4, and moved on to the quick silvery prose of George Berkeley. The name of Thomas Reid was never mentioned; I didn't learn about him until years later.

As to how history of philosophy was done, I have often cited O. K. Bouwsma's articles on Descartes as paradigmatic of the lot: thoughts that occurred to me one day when reading a couple of sentences in an English translation of Descartes's *Meditations*. The course I took from Werner Jaeger in the classics department, on Gregory of Nyssa, was different; this was German philology and historicism at its finest. And the course I took from Harry Wolfson on Spinoza was different. We never got beyond Proposition X in the *Ethics*; whenever we turned to a new proposition, Wolfson argued that it could not be understood without understanding its background in the whole tradition of Jewish thought, beginning with Philo. To this day I probably know as much about Philo as about Spinoza.

For reasons not entirely clear to me, either then or now, I did not want to hang around as a graduate student. So after the requisite two years of course work, I settled quickly on a dissertation topic, "Whitehead's Theory of Individuation," and spent my third year writing the dissertation. In one of D. C. Williams's courses, I had read some of the things Whitehead published early in his career as a philosopher and was enraptured. Now I had to deal with *Process and Reality*. That disillusioned me with Whitehead; I found his writings too lacking in rigor. I have not looked at the dissertation since turning it in. My book *On Universals*, however, was my own attempt to treat what Whitehead called "eternal objects."

Sometime in the course of my third year, D. C. Williams urged me to apply for the Sheldon Traveling Fellowship. When I looked up the stipulations for the fellowship, I discovered that it was designed to support those whose dissertation topic required that they do research abroad. I called Williams's attention to the fact that everything Whitehead had published was readily available at Harvard; and that, in any case, I hoped to have my dissertation finished by the end of the summer. Williams said that didn't matter. So I applied and received one of the fellowships. The dean of Arts and Sciences, the classicist J. P. Elder, held a little sherry party for the six of us who received the fellowship that year. He knew the plight I was in, that my thesis did not require doing research abroad. So he tapped me on the shoulder and said, "Wolterstorff, you must use this money to sample European culture"— those were his exact words; I remember them well. My immediate thought was, if Harvard wants to pay me to sample European culture, who am I, a young kid from the farm country of Minnesota who used to milk cows, feed pigs, and herd cattle on horseback—that's all true— who am I to tell them that there are better ways for them to spend their money?

So my wife and I and our infant daughter set off for Cambridge in the fall of '56 to sample European culture. I listened to John Wisdom lecturing with mock agony, and I had tea with C. D. Broad in his rooms. Broad told me that he thought the reason Calvin College produced so many philosophers was that there was an intrinsic affinity between Reformed theology and philosophy. He also told me that fishermen speaking Frisian and fishermen speaking English were able to communicate with each other. I had read much of Broad's work on metaphysics and had some questions to ask. He gave me to believe that it was impolite to discuss such matters over tea.

In the spring, while still in Europe, I received a letter from Brand Blanshard, chair of the philosophy department at Yale, offering me a position as instructor in philosophy at Yale. Not inviting me to apply but offering me a position. I accepted. Blanshard proved, when I met him, to be a courtly gentleman, and I never got up the courage to ask him how this had all gone. But I'm quite sure I know; it was not unusual in those days. He called up the chair at Harvard, asked whether they had any recent graduates Yale could hire, the chair at Harvard said, "Sure; try Wolterstorff," and that was it. In short, the old boys' network doing its work. I am now embarrassed that I should have been the beneficiary of this system; at the time, I was unabashedly delighted.

It was at Yale that first year that I had what remains the worst teaching experience of my entire career. Dick Bernstein had taught a very successful course in philosophy the preceding year to patients at the Yale Psychiatric Institute. Dick was now on sabbatical to Israel. I received a call from someone at the institute asking whether I would teach the course. I needed the money—my Yale salary was $4,000—so I said yes. I decided that I would follow Dick's example and offer an introduction to the great figures of Western philosophy, one day a week for ten weeks.

I arrived for the first session and was led into a large gymnasium-like space. There were ten or twelve metal chairs set up in a circle in the middle; thick mats were spread around the room. The patients came in, took chairs, and the attendant locked us in the room. Just as I was ready to begin, one of the patients got up, dragged one of the mats into the middle of the circle of chairs, and laid down on his back on the mat. I was well into giving an enthusiastic explanation of Plato's theory of forms—the bed itself, outside of time, taking up no space, unchange-able, pure bed, bed all the way down, very bed of very bed, that sort of thing—when the patient on the mat suddenly bolted upright and with a tone of total incredulity in his voice exclaimed, "Plato said *what*? He said *what*?" Suddenly my world began to tilt and totter. "Who are the crazies here?" I toiled on, trying now to make Plato sound quite ordinary, but the wind was out of my sails.

On the way home, thoroughly depressed, reflecting that I still had nine sessions to go, I found myself reviewing the syllabus. Aristotle next week. Rather boring but shouldn't cause any problems. Then, Descartes. "No, not Descartes. Doubting the existence of an external world!" Then and there I decided to play the coward. I would tell them that there had been a change in the syllabus. We could not possibly cover all the significant Western philosophers; I had decided to skip Descartes.

II

My aim has been to draw a picture of a bygone era in all its strangeness—strangeness for those of you under fifty. It's been rather like a
catalogue so far, and if I continue in this vein, my talk will shortly
become as boring as we found Locke's droning on about ideas. So let
me try to describe the philosophical ethos of Harvard in those days.
What was shaping this particular manifestation of the philosophical enterprise?

The final days of logical positivism, that's what was shaping the enterprise. I take the core of logical positivism to have been the conviction
that science is that component in present-day culture which harbors the
greatest promise for the future of humankind. If one is a philosopher
holding that conviction, one of the challenges confronting one is to
explain how science, the good stuff, is to be differentiated from all the
other things rather like it. That was the so-called problem of demarcation. The positivists, as we all know, tried to demarcate science by
reference to defining features of the language of science; logical positivism in its classical form held that a defining feature of a scientific claim
is that it is empirically verifiable. Already in my day that particular
proposal was regarded as shaky; for one thing, Karl Popper had offered
his disconfirmation proposal. Nonetheless, we talked readily and easily
about *the* logic of science. It was assumed that the formal logic of
science was some combination of the symbolic logic that we were being
taught, plus probability theory, and that genuine scientific theories
were somehow hooked up logically with "sense reports," as they were
often called. Remember, this was before the publication of Kuhn's
Structure of Scientific Revolutions. The challenge was to say just how
theories were hooked up to sense reports.

It was acknowledged that science, as it actually occurs, often does
not appear to have the sense-based structure that we as philosophers
knew it must have; its structure was hidden. It was thus the business of
the philosopher of science to reveal the hidden. That was mind-crack-
ingly difficult: only the best and the brightest were up to it. In my day,
we talked endlessly about the problem of counterfactuals. Science as it
actually occurs uses counterfactuals with abandon. It was hard to discern the logic behind these counterfactuals; they resisted truth-func-
tional analysis.

Earlier, I mentioned that, whereas metaethics was all the rage, meta-epistemology did not exist. Offhand that seems strange: if there's the one, why not the other? Once one sees that logical positivism was the background, it all falls into place. We knew the structure of that really good stuff which is scientific knowledge; its structure is classical foundationalism of some sort, though nobody at the time identified it as such. Thus, no need for meta-epistemology. But the status of ethical language was deeply problematic within the positivist system. That's why all the talk about metaethics and why that talk took the specific form of worrying about the nature of the language of ethics.

What was the business of philosophy itself within this scheme? The business of philosophy was said to be conceptual analysis—to which should be added, analysis and appraisal of arguments. Philosophers are specialists in concepts and arguments. "What is it" questions preoccupied us: "What is art?" "What is science?" "What is knowledge?" It was as if Socrates had been resurrected and become legion.

Analysis of the concepts and arguments of science, and appraisal of those arguments, received priority, but there was nothing wrong with moving out from science to other fields. I mentioned that I stayed away from the aesthetics course because it seemed little more than armchair psychologizing. Monroe Beardsley's *Aesthetics*, appearing a few years later in 1958, was a bolt of analytic light into the darkness. Beardsley argued that the topic of philosophical aesthetics is not art but talk about art by art critics; the philosopher analyzes the concepts and arguments of the critics and appraises their arguments. Thus did Beardsley fit aesthetics into the dominant philosophical ethos; aesthetics then took off.

In retrospect, I see that this whole way of thinking of philosophy and of its relation to the other disciplines was very much in the Kantian tradition: the business of natural science is the contingent, the business of philosophy is the necessary. (Mathematics is akin to philosophy in this scheme.) My own view is that one of the reasons Continental philosophy parted ways from analytic philosophy sometime after Husserl is that the Continentals embraced the Hegelian notion of historical dialectic; a few philosophers advance the dialectic, the others comment on the advances. We at Harvard were definitely not into historical dialectic.

I did not mention that in my days as a graduate student at Harvard there were no such things as feminist studies, African American studies, or any other such perspectival studies. Had anyone at the time proposed any such study, they would have been greeted with blank incomprehension. Had an explanation been offered, the response would have been that any such study would be a biased study and hence had no place in the academy. The enterprise of academic learning was seen as a generically human enterprise. It's not hard to see why. Conceptual analysis and the analysis and appraisal of arguments: what does that have to do with being a woman or being an African American? It's a generically human enterprise. Likewise, hooking up scientific theories to sense reports in the right way: what does that have to do with being gay or being Buddhist? It, too, is a generically human enterprise.

I should mention that the philosophical ethos at Yale when I taught there at the beginning of my career was very different from that at Harvard. At Yale, British idealism in its final manifestation was trying to fend off analytic philosophy.

III

Philosophy today is profoundly different from what it was at Harvard fifty years ago. What accounts for the difference?

I suggested that it was logical positivism in its final days that was shaping the philosophical enterprise at Harvard. John Wild was then teaching at Harvard, and he was certainly not a logical positivist or even an analytic philosopher. He started a little reading group in which we went through the manuscript of the first English translation of Heidegger's *Being and Time*; Bert Dreyfus was a member of the group. And the attitude of D. C. Williams toward logical positivism always seemed to me one of bemusement. But positivism in its final days shaped the enterprise as a whole.

Winds of change were beginning to blow, however; Oxford "ordinary language philosophy" was the new thing, and people were beginning to read late Wittgenstein. Paul Ziff was calling Wittgenstein's *Investigations* "*Prolegomena to Any Future Metaphysics.*" Quine returned from his year at Oxford with the quip that whenever henceforth he heard "ordinary language," he would think of Oxford. In my third year, J. L.

Austin came to teach a seminar and give the lectures that became *How to Do Things with Words*. He participated in a public debate on determinism with the behaviorist psychologist B. F. Skinner; it was as classic a case of ships passing in the dark as anything ever was. Skinner talked about what his rats could and could not do; Austin insisted that the way Skinner was using the words "could" and "could not" was not the way one would use them in ordinary language. For a brief time, I was enraptured by this new development; I too talked of what one would and would not say. In his comments on a paper I wrote for him, D. C. Williams said that he discerned the slimy trail of the linguistic serpent across its pages.

Ordinary-language philosophy turned its back on the scientism that was determinative of logical positivism; that was evident to me at the time, and I found it liberating. But I now see that ordinary-language philosophy perpetuated other themes in positivism. It perpetuated the preoccupation with language, obviously. And it perpetuated positivism's understanding of philosophy as exercising a policing function, telling us what can and cannot be said. I think the demise of this policing function goes a long way toward accounting for the difference between philosophy then and philosophy now. There's nobody doing any serious policing nowadays in analytic philosophy. Those who think all truths must have truth makers do talk about "catching cheaters." But so far as I can tell, this is all rather playful; nobody concedes that he's been caught.

Let me develop a bit this point about policing. A persistent topic in classical modern philosophy, from John Locke onwards, was that of the limits of thought and judgment; it was regularly asserted or assumed that if we could understand the origin and function of concepts, we would then be in a position to discern those limits. In Kant, especially, views on the origin and function of concepts were a crucial ingredient in his view as to the limits of the thinkable. Logical positivism, with its criterion of meaning, and ordinary-language philosophy, with its talk about what one would and would not say, were a continuation, each in its own way, of this traditional topic of the limits of thought and judgment.

A consequence of the demise of logical positivism and of ordinary-language philosophy has proved to be that the general topic of limits has lost all interest for philosophers in the analytic tradition. Analytic philosophers do still charge people with failing to make a genuine judgment or think a genuine thought. But the tacit assumption is that such claims have to be defended on an ad hoc basis; skepticism reigns among analytic philosophers concerning all grand proposals for demarcating the thinkable from the unthinkable, the assertible from the non-assertible. That's what I meant when I said that analytic philosophers are no longer doing any serious policing.

I think it was the demise of the policing function within analytic philosophy that made possible the extraordinary flourishing in recent years of metaphysics, of philosophy of religion, and of philosophical theology—in particular, of philosophical theology that is theistically realist in its orientation. There's nobody around telling the metaphysicians, the philosophers of religion, and the philosophical theologians that their utterances lack sense. These developments have contributed, in turn, to the resurgence of interest in medieval philosophy. No longer is the metaphysics or theology of the medieval philosophers dismissed on the ground that they were trying to think the unthinkable or say the unsayable. My guess is that the demise of the policing function also goes a long way toward accounting for the fact that ethics today is a vastly richer, less uptight field of inquiry than it was in my grad-school days and that aesthetics also is.

One of the consequences or corollaries of the demise of the policing function has been the simultaneous collapse of the old, Kantian-style distinction between philosophy and the other *Wissenschaften*. The idea in my grad-school days was that philosophers can't talk about God but only about God-talk, can't talk about art but only about art-talk, can't talk about history but only about history-talk, and so forth down the line. Thank God that's all gone.

Almost as important in accounting for why philosophy today is so different from philosophy then was the emergence of the new philosophy of science and of meta-epistemology. By the new philosophy of science, I mean philosophy of science which is seriously interested in how science actually works, rather than approaching science with classical foundationalist preconceptions as to how it *must* work and then trying to show that, in spite of appearances, it really does work that way. Whatever you and I may want to say today about the ambiguities, lack of rigor, rhetorical excess, and so forth in the work of Kuhn, Feyerabend, and their cohorts, its effect on us at the time cannot be exaggerated.

I think the emergence of meta-epistemology has to be seen as part of the same post-positivist development. The difficulties the positivists had experienced in working out their classical-foundationalist preconceptions provoked the search for alternatives, and thereby the conscious awareness, lacking in my epistemology course, of classical foundationalism as just one among many options. Shortly, Quine started talking in coherentist fashion about "the web of belief."

And what accounts for the fact that history of philosophy is so different today from what it was then? Until not long ago, it was characteristic of us in the analytic tradition of philosophy to think of the history of philosophy in terms of *problems*. Our courses and our textbooks were all set up that way. In aesthetics, one had the problem of representation, the problem of expression, the problem of truth in art, the problem of what is art, and so forth. We talked about these problems as if they existed in some Platonic realm of forms. History was irrelevant to the problems themselves. The only brush of philosophical problems with history was that each was discovered at a certain time and received proposed solutions at various times.

The problems were of course *our* problems. All the historical philosophers were treated as if they were twentieth-century analytic philosophers born out of season, discussing the same problems, albeit often rather clumsily and in goofy language. Plato and Nelson Goodman were side by side in the anthologies discussing the problem of representation in art; Aristotle and Roderick Chisholm were side by side discussing the problem of what is knowledge. Everything was decontextualized. The classical logical positivists seem to have assumed that they themselves were the discoverers of the problems they were interested in or that nobody before them had given answers still worth discussing; hence, they themselves had no interest in the history of philosophy whatsoever.

In recent years, there has been an extraordinary flowering of interest among analytic philosophers in the history of philosophy. The history that has emerged is very different from that which earlier analytic philosophers wrote. Our historians now regularly attend to the contexts within which historical figures conducted their reflections, taking the relevant context to be much more than just what other philosophers were saying. And rather than assuming that the historical figures must have been discussing our problems, our historians try to get inside the ways of thinking of the historical figures to discover their problems and why they saw them as problems. The results have been rich, fascinating, illuminating, and provocative—one of the great periods in the writing of the history of philosophy.

How did this development come about? What explains it? I don't fully know. But let me mention two developments that I think have contributed. For one thing—and now I begin to repeat myself—the demise of the policing function played a role. In my own book on Locke, I argued that Locke has to be understood as an anxiety figure; Locke was almost always dealing with the anxieties evoked by the recent breakup of the religious unity of Europe and the warfare that resulted. In an earlier day, a good many of my fellow philosophers would have said that my talk about social and cultural anxiety wasn't really philosophy; when I wrote the book, in the nineties, it never occurred to me to worry about that response.

A second development that I think contributed to the new history of philosophy has been in the background of my discussion for quite some time now, but I have not called attention to it. Logical positivism was a highly programmatic development in philosophy, as was ordinary-language philosophy. After the demise of those two programs, we haven't had any big programs in analytic philosophy—small, localized programs but no big, overarching programs. Sometimes when I talk about this to present-day grad students, they express nostalgia for the excitement that surrounds a big program. Well, yes, those were exciting days. But the point I want to make here is that the absence of any big program has made it easier for the historians among us to get into the mentality of historical figures rather than squeezing them into our mentality.

I seem to be falling into a cataloguing mode again. So after briefly taking note of one more development that helps to explain why philosophy today is so different from what it was then, I'm going to call this off. My days in grad school were before the assassination of J. F. Kennedy, before the Vietnam War, before the civil rights movement, before Sputnik, before the feminist movement, before Watergate, before the landing on the moon, before *Roe v. Wade*. American society has gone through enormous social and cultural changes between then and now, and philosophy has responded to those changes. Those changes go a long way toward explaining the rise of interest in political philosophy. They go a long way toward explaining why philosophy of science is no longer the premier subdiscipline within philosophy; nobody believes any more that science will save us. And they go a long way toward explaining the emergence of explicitly perspectival approaches within the academy in general and philosophy in particular. As increasing numbers of women entered philosophy, they became emboldened to say that what was represented as being generically human scholarship did not look generic to them.

IV

I have been speaking as an observer of the scene. Now I come to the awkward part: saying something about my own philosophical work and its relation to these developments.

I did my undergraduate work at Calvin College, Calvin being an institution sponsored by a denomination in the Dutch Reformed tradition of Protestantism. Al Plantinga was one of my classmates. We became friends and have remained dear friends ever since. I have learned more from him about philosophy than from anyone else—with the possible exception of Thomas Reid.

Everybody was required to take a couple of courses in philosophy. I signed up for philosophy in the first semester of my sophomore year. The instructor was a superb teacher and fine philosopher, Henry Stob. About thirty minutes into the first class session, I said to myself, "I have no idea whether I'll be any good at this stuff, but if I am, this is it." I see it as of yesterday. Philosophy chose me; I didn't choose philosophy.

Another of our philosophy professors, Harry Jellema, was the most charismatic teacher I have ever had. Jellema wrote very little, and in what he did write, none of his charisma comes through. He violated almost every rule for good teaching. He always came late. He had no syllabus. His assignments were never clear. His exams were unpredictable. But he was the most gripping teacher I have ever had. I took almost all of his courses. One year, Al Plantinga and I were the only students in Jellema's course on Kant's *Pure Critique*. Apparently, the college had no rules in those days about minimum class size. Both Al and I had a copy of the *Critique* in its original German along with the Norman Kemp Smith translation. We went carefully through the text, getting through roughly the first third of it by the end of the semester. In a course I had from Stob, the text was Aquinas's *Summa theologiae*.

Again, we went carefully through the text, arriving at question 21 of the first book by the end of the semester. It was in these courses that I learned that good philosophy is slow.

From my teachers at Calvin, I imbibed a picture of what philosophy is. A description I once heard attributed to Wilfrid Sellars puts it well: philosophy asks how every thing, in the most general sense of "thing," hangs together, in the most general sense of "hangs together." I also imbibed an understanding of how to engage the philosophical tradition, past and present. Don't just look at the problems a philosopher discusses and the answers the philosopher gives to those problems. Dig down to the philosopher's underlying way of thinking, its assumptions and motivations. Why is the philosopher asking these questions? Why is the philosopher asking them this way? Why does the philosopher think them important? Why do philosophers give the answers they do? And I imbibed a non-foundationalist way of understanding how a philosopher arrives at a way of thinking and works it out. Any philosophers worth their salt will give lots of arguments. But arguments in support of what a philosopher believes will inevitably run out at some point. Philosophy, at bottom, is a perspectival enterprise.

I likewise imbibed a sense of the role of religion in philosophy. Philosophers, in working out how everything hangs together, often stake out positions on issues on which one or another religion also has a position. Philosophy in that way is not religiously neutral; it carries religious import. The attempt to get philosophy and religion out of each other's hair and keep them out presupposes a false understanding of religion or philosophy or both. I imbibed a tacit understanding of the place of religion in human existence. Religion, rather than being a sign of malformation or malfunctioning, is natural to human beings; atheism is what needs explaining. Religion is not going to disappear. I imbibed an understanding of how my identity as a Christian believer should relate to my work as a philosopher. My Christian convictions should enter into the mix of what's relevant as I participate with my fellow philosophers in the enterprise of trying to figure out how everything hangs together. And lastly, I imbibed the conviction that to be entitled to bring one's religious convictions into the mix when trying to figure out how everything hangs together, one did not first have to support those convictions with arguments. You can see here the origins of Reformed epistemology. I myself have always believed that we human beings and this physical world in which we find ourselves are the handiwork of some being quite other. I have tried on occasion to get into the mindset of believing it all just happened. It works for a little while. But then I take note of the immensity, the minuteness, the intricacy, the fine-tuning, the beauty and glory of it all, and I ineluctably snap out of it. No argument there. But that's OK.

This comprehensive understanding of philosophy, religion, and their relation that I imbibed from my college teachers has come to shape my work in philosophy. I need scarcely say that it fits far better with philosophy as practiced and understood today than with philosophy as it was practiced and understood in my grad-student days. Then it was eccentric. I joined everybody else in talking about the verifiability criterion and counterfactuals, but at the same time, I was asking myself, "Why are we all talking about the verifiability criterion and counterfactuals? Why is this important?" The understanding I just sketched of philosophy, religion, and their relationship is by no means a consensus understanding today, but neither is it eccentric.

I said just above that the understanding I imbibed from my college teachers "has come to shape" my work in philosophy. By that turn of phrase, I meant to suggest that not all of it has always shaped my work. My early work in philosophy was very much in the ahistorical mode of the classic analytic philosopher. As I recall, it was my work in aesthetics that first jolted me out of that.

I was as enraptured as anybody by the appearance of Beardsley's *Aesthetics*. Now, at last, aesthetics could take its place as a genuinely philosophical enterprise instead of languishing as a branch of lay psychology. For several years, I used Beardsley's book as a text in teaching aesthetics, supplementing it with an anthology laid out in classic problems form. I discussed Plato's definition of art, Tolstoy's definition of art, Collingwood's definition of art, Kant's definition of the aesthetic, Beardsley's definition of the aesthetic, and so forth.

Then doubts began to set in on a number of fronts. Beardsley and the other contemporary writers I was reading argued that art is for aesthetic delight and assumed that aesthetic delight requires leisure; I went along. But then one day, the University of Michigan radio station played a recording of work songs from around the world, and the obvious thought occurred to me that though I was listening to these songs at my leisure, their original function was not to occupy one's leisure but to accompany work. Around the same time, it occurred to me that the elevation of the aesthetic in art implied a demotion of liturgical art and memorial art, and that seemed mistaken to me.

It took me a decade or more to figure out what was going on; in retrospect, it seems blindingly obvious. I now think that almost all writing about art over the past two centuries by Western intellectuals and academics represents a way of thinking about the arts that emerged in the eighteenth century; writing about the arts consists in good measure of articulating this way of thinking, legitimating it, applying it, etc. I had not seen it that way. I had not seen it as a historically contingent way of thinking to which there are alternatives, but as the natural human way of thinking about art. That was the assumption that I now identified and began to question. I found myself compelled to back up and ask where this way of thinking emerged, why it emerged, what its underlying assumptions were, why it was thought so important to differentiate art from crafts, aesthetic experience from other kinds of experience, why people placed their religious hopes in art, and so forth. I became convinced that only when I had understood this way of thinking, along with its origins and assumptions, could I appraise it and go on to work out my own systematics, for systematic aesthetics had been and remained my goal.

I began to teach aesthetics in accord with these convictions. I discarded the problems-oriented textbooks and tried to cultivate in students self-awareness concerning the way they thought about the arts. Not all students liked this approach. For some, art as they thought about it and as it's been thought about for these past two centuries was very precious. They didn't want me explaining that way of thinking as historically contingent and holding it up to the light of day; they wanted me to articulate, legitimate, and apply it.

This way of approaching philosophical topics has come to characterize much of what I have written in recent years in areas other than aesthetics; my systematic endeavors are embedded within a historical narrative. I do indeed want to know whether it's true that to be entitled to hold beliefs about God one must hold those beliefs for reasons. But before I plunge into the systematics of that issue, I want to understand the way of thinking about reason and religion within which this claim occurs and the historical origins of that way of thinking. For it is a historically contingent way of thinking; it's not a way of thinking that one finds among the ancient or medieval philosophers. So also, I do indeed want to know whether Rawls is right in his claim that in a liberal democracy we must stand ready to support the positions we take on matters of basic justice by arguments whose premises are drawn from public reason. But before I plunge into the systematics of that issue, I want to understand the way of thinking within which this claim occurs and what it was that gave rise to this way of thinking. For it, too, is a historically contingent way of thinking; it's not part of humankind's patrimony. You may think that conceptual analysis is the entire business of philosophy. Fair enough. But I want to know what is the way of thinking within which this view of philosophy occurred and what led to that way of thinking. It's not just the obvious truth of the matter.

To this day, I do not fully understand why I found it so gripping to read Thomas Reid for the first time. Partly it was his anti-foundationalism; trust, not certitude, does and must lie at the bottom of our human existence. But I think it was also that I found Reid to be a soul brother in the way of going about philosophy that I was moving toward. Rather than just plunging ahead and dealing with the problems then on the plate of epistemologists, Reid identified the way of thinking that lay behind those problems—"the way of ideas," he called it. Having identified that way of thinking, he subjected it to withering critique; only then did he move on to develop his own epistemological systematics in an entirely new direction.

I do not believe that the problems we philosophers deal with are lodged in some Platonic heaven and that their only brush with history is getting discovered at a certain time and receiving proposed solutions at certain times. They occur within ways of thinking. And those ways of thinking come from somewhere. They are motivated by developments of many different sorts: social anxieties, social hopes, cultural confusions, developments in the arts, feats of philosophical imagination, developments in religion.

Analytic philosophy is regularly accused of sterile logic-chopping, of being divorced from the real questions of real human beings. I don't doubt that some of it is that. But mostly, it only appears divorced from the real questions of real human beings. Partly it appears that way because it's been the habit of analytic philosophers to ignore the ways of thinking that constitute the context of their philosophical problems and the concerns that gave rise to those ways of thinking; partly it appears that way because it is the habit of the analytic philosopher to stick far more closely to the cases than most modes of philosophizing do, being wary of making generalizations that don't fit the cases.

It was rather late in my career that I first read the great turn-of-the-last-century German sociologist, Max Weber; but it's now clear to me that I have unwittingly spent a good deal of my life in philosophy attacking the Weber paradigm of life in modernity. One of Weber's famous theses, as you know, was that a hallmark of a modernized society is that social life is differentiated into distinct sectors, with life within each sector shaped by whatever be the organizing value of that sector. Life within each sector has become, in that way, autonomous. Art comes into its own when a distinct art world emerges, with life within that world shaped by aesthetic values and freed from influence by other sectors and their values. *Wissenschaft* comes into its own when a distinct academic world emerges, with life within that world shaped by intellectual values and freed from influence by other sectors and their values. And as for religion, it gets squeezed out of all these sectors and into our private lives; there is no place for the religious voice in the public sectors of society.

I've been arguing that Weber is mostly wrong about this. It's possible in a rough and ready way to identify Weber's differentiated spheres. But we will not understand art if we think that in the modern world art is shaped only by aesthetic values, impervious to developments in wider society and culture. We will not understand philosophy if we think that in the modern world philosophy is shaped only by intellectual values, impervious to our human hopes and fears, aspirations and anxieties. And we will not understand much of anything about the modern world or religion if we think that religion in the modern world has retreated into the private.

I have run out of time. To my great regret, I have not had a chance to say anything at all about the two wonderful institutions in which I have done most of my teaching, Calvin College and Yale University, about the colleagues with whom I have taught, or about the students whom I have taught. I have not had a chance to describe the weekly philosophy colloquia that we had at Calvin College when I was teaching there. It was in those colloquia that I learned how to be a philosopher— how to combine vision with craftsmanship. Nor have I had a chance to describe those summer evenings when Al Plantinga and I were both teaching at Calvin, and O. K. Bouwsma would invite us over to his vacation house to talk philosophy and O. K. would trap Al into saying truly dumb things, each year again. They say that horses don't bump their heads on the same beam twice.

To have lived through the changes in philosophy that I have described has been fascinating; to have made some contribution to those changes has been deeply gratifying. My life in philosophy has been a wonderful life. Many of you here have contributed to making it that. For that, I thank you with all my heart.

NOTE

John Dewey Lecture delivered before the 104th annual Central Division Meeting of the American Philosophical Association in Chicago, Illinois, on April 21, 2006. Used by permission of the John Dewey Foundation.

2

SIXTY YEARS OF PHILOSOPHY IN A LIFE

J. B. Schneewind

I

I was born in 1930 in a large town in Westchester. My parents were secularized American Jews from families long settled in the States. They were solid Roosevelt Democrats but not active politically. My father worked for a large corporation in Manhattan, my mother raised my sister and me and then, during the Second World War, took up substitute teaching. Shortly after my birth, we moved to Pelham Manor. It was a pleasant little suburb of tree-lined streets and separate houses surrounded by well-kept lawns and filled with white Christians. They were mostly Protestant and mostly anti-Semitic. My parents learned that they couldn't join the country club. I learned that I couldn't play with all the other kids. From time to time, I was chased home from school by boys throwing stones and shouting "dirty Jew." Boys I thought were friends had birthday parties to which I wasn't invited. There was a dancing class to which I couldn't go. Compared to what was being done to Jews in Europe, this was completely trivial. But it made me aware that I was an outsider, excluded from whatever it was that the Christian kids shared.

One thing they shared was something called Sunday school. They were not available on Sunday mornings. I'd see them going into their churches, the boys in jackets and neckties, but I didn't know what they did there. I belonged to no formal religious group. There were one or two other Jewish families in Pelham Manor, but there was no synagogue, and my parents would not have sent me had there been one. I had no formal religious education until I was a teenager, when I was sent, along with a few other Jewish religious illiterates, to a Bible reading group run by a believing Jew. But early on, I learned from miscellaneous reading that one thing Christians were taught in Sunday school was that they were to love one another.

I could not put this teaching together with what I knew of how my schoolmates acted and of what Germans—presumably Christians—were doing to Jews in Europe. During the war, my mother's father had helped get some of our European relatives to the States, and we had them to dinner from time to time. Their presence made the persecution of the Jews more vivid than the newspapers did. But they did not talk about their plight, still less how Christianity was involved in it. Even after Laura Hobson's 1947 novel, *Gentleman's Agreement*, made American anti-Semitism discussable, I heard no one try to explain how a religion of love could cause such hatred.

I was not raised in any religion, and I've never had any religious beliefs. Am I an atheist or an agnostic? It would be more accurate to say that I am just not interested in assessing religious claims to truth. I've read many Victorian sermons and a fair amount of Christian theology. But I have not been looking for a faith I could accept. My aim has been only to understand how religion and morality have affected each other. My early experiences of exclusion in Pelham Manor led me to stay away from religion of any variety. It's always been morality that interested me first.

My interest in philosophical ethics and in the relations between religion and morality is largely due, I think, to my experiences of being an outsider because of a religious moral teaching whose workings I could not understand. I cannot be sure that this was what made me a philosopher. But it certainly left me with questions. Religious believers sometimes ask whether anyone can be moral without religion. If in my childhood I could have thought in such abstract terms, I would have asked instead: how can anyone be moral *with* religion? Either question can seem outrageous to partisans of one side or the other. Between them, they point to issues that have concerned me all my life.

Eventually, I came to feel strongly about other issues as well. I didn't experience economic hardship or notice racial prejudice during my childhood. It was only later that I became aware of the injustices to which poverty and race give rise. If I have come to be moved by these issues, it has been because anti-Semitism first taught me that however smooth the social surface may seem, there are terrible things going on beneath it. Being Jewish makes me feel that I share to some extent in the vulnerabilities of the oppressed.

In the early 1930s, Robert Hutchins, the new president of the University of Chicago, paid a visit to John Grier Hibben, a philosopher who was then president of Princeton. Hutchins asked how many Jewish students Princeton had; Hibben told him there were about two hundred. Hutchins writes that he then

> asked about the number the year before. Hibben responded: "About two hundred." I said that was very odd and asked how it happened. He said he didn't know; it just happened. Mrs. Hibben was outraged and said, "Jack Hibben, I don't see how you can sit there and lie to this young man. You know very well that you and Dean Eisenhart get together every year and fix the quota."[1]

—the quota that kept the number of Jews so steady.

Jewish quotas were introduced in the 1920s by the president of Harvard, A. Lawrence Lowell. One of the main changes in academia since I entered it has been their disappearance and the coming of large numbers of Jews, as students, teachers, and administrators. I wish that academe had done as well with racial minority members and with women. There are many more of both now than there were in 1947, but philosophy as a field has lagged behind other disciplines. Despite this, women and African Americans have become noticeable and notable contributors to philosophy. That's a second major and happy change I've lived through.

In 1947, however, when I applied for admission, Harvard still had a Jewish quota. There's some evidence that the quota kept me out. I went instead to Cornell. And that is where philosophy entered my life.

I had never given the subject any thought. In high school, I read Thoreau's *Walden* and was cheered by its encouragement of individuality, but I read nothing else even remotely philosophical. During my freshman year, I took no philosophy courses. I went to Cornell intending to be a chemist. In my first chemistry course, however, the woman who was my lab partner lost patience with me. My clumsiness, she said—quite rightly—was wrecking our lab work; I should go away and just use her results. While I was realizing my scientific ineptitude, I was reading the book of Job for a literature course. That led me to write a term paper on the problem of evil. I was fascinated by the conceptual issues (as I later learned to call them). Next term, I applied for an experimental tutorial program started by, among others, Max Black. The applicants were told that it did not matter what they majored in, as everyone would take the same courses. Many applicants wanted to major in literature, only a handful in philosophy. So I said, opportunistically, that I'd be a philosophy major. I was accepted as such, and in the autumn of 1948, I took my first philosophy course. It was on moral philosophy; it was taught by Stuart Brown, and in it, I read Kant's *Groundwork* for the first time. I didn't understand it, and I've been struggling with it ever since. But I could see even then that it was addressing my concerns about the relations between morality and religion. I began to think that my decision to major in philosophy was luckier than I could have hoped.

I explored the subject with growing ardor. A third or more of my work was in philosophy courses. In my senior year, I had a graduate seminar with Brown on the British moralists, another with Arthur Murphy on recent ethics, and a reading course, again with Murphy, on Kant. I studied history of philosophy with Gregory Vlastos. With him and with Mario Einaudi I studied the history of political thought. Students were urged to get help from George Sabine's *History of Political Thought*, and I did find it useful. Naturally I looked for a comparable history of moral philosophy. But, except for Sidgwick's *Short History of Ethics*, I could find nothing of the same caliber. Sabine's book remained in my mind even though I moved away from taking it as a model.

At Cornell I did logic and philosophy of language with Max Black. He was my advisor. I lived in dread of him. He was often cruel and cutting in his remarks to students. Nonetheless, he was a most effective teacher. I learned far more about writing from him than from the required writing course. I was not good at logic—not at all—but out of pure terror I did well even in Black's advanced logic class. I had occasional nightmares about him for the next twenty years.

The few philosophy majors were a congenial group. I got to know some of the graduate students as well, in particular Bill Gass, who had not yet begun writing fiction. And I started going to the departmental colloquium. One day, during my junior year, it was attended by an elderly man in a plaid shirt. I thought perhaps he was the father of a faculty member. After a paper, there was silence. Finally, the elderly man started to talk. He went on for about half an hour; I couldn't really follow his remarks, but I noticed that Black had not lit his usual cigar and that everyone was listening attentively. After the stranger stopped, Black said: "Professor Wittgenstein just suggested that . . ." I'd heard that name, though I knew nothing about him. (This was before the publication of *Philosophical Investigations*.) As we left after the discussion, Black turned to me and said, ponderously, "Remember this meeting, my boy."

Aside from the philosophers, the student with whom I spent most time was one I'd met early in 1948, Harold Bloom. We became close friends. I'd made the mistake of joining a fraternity, and I lived in the fraternity house during my sophomore year. Despite that, I spent most of my time with Bloom. He was in the tutorial program, and we had many classes together. During our junior and senior years, we roomed together. He made me glad I was not studying literature. Bloom could read at an astonishing pace, with total recall; he remembered fully every poem he liked, including *Paradise Lost*; he scribbled off his term papers nonstop in longhand and sent them to his sister to be typed without revising, and the papers kept winning prizes. At one point, I was reading Popper, and he was reading St. John of the Cross. One Friday evening, we started arguing about rationalism and mysticism. By Sunday afternoon, we decided to go to a movie to take a break. Then we got tossed out of the theater because we couldn't stop arguing. I learned an enormous amount from Harold. After we graduated, we kept on seeing one another for years, still arguing. But he went on to Yale and I to Princeton.

II

Before getting to Princeton, I'd had to explain to my parents that I was intending to become a philosophy professor. My father had not gone to college; my mother went only long enough to get a teacher's license. They had no idea of what philosophy was, and I could explain neither it nor my fascination with it to them—nor, indeed, to myself. My father asked if I could earn a living at it. I could only reply that Max Black earned enough to support a family, so I supposed I might do so too. With some bemusement, but no hesitation, my parents backed my decision and supplied enough money to supplement the meager fellowship I'd been offered.

Princeton was still a men's school when I arrived in 1951; chapel was still required of undergrads; the Graduate College, known as Goon Castle, was a long walk from the meager opportunities for relaxation that the village offered; and New York City was too distant and too expensive to be any help. The philosophy department was at a low point in its history. I did not find there teachers as good as those I'd had at Cornell. But Princeton was not all a disappointment. It was there that I first saw wisteria in full bloom and there that I met Rogers Albritton.

The wisteria grew on the walls of the Graduate College; its fragrance attracted bees in the daytime and lonely graduate students in the evening. A love of wisteria has stayed with me ever since. And so has the effect of knowing Rogers Albritton. He was still a graduate student but, even then, the magical philosophical interlocutor that I—and everyone else—found him to be in later years. He seemed able to divine my philosophical perplexities before I knew what they were and to go a long way toward untangling or just getting rid of them. He attended all the sessions of a seminar on sense data that Norman Malcolm gave, as a visiting professor. Rogers and Norman debated intensively and unforgettably. Each week, Rogers challenged some point Norman wanted to insist on. When Norman couldn't reply, he'd say: "I'll have to think about that." Then the next week, he'd give an answer. He plainly had thought about the challenge. The two of them provided a model of protracted, acute philosophical debate. I got, for the first time, some real understanding of how attention to language could have important philosophical payoffs. Between them, they demolished sense-datum theory.

When I started at Princeton, there were only three other entering doctoral students in philosophy and not a large number ahead of us. John Rawls had finished his dissertation just before I arrived but was still there, as an instructor for undergraduates. Despite his great personal modesty, he already had an awe-inspiring reputation. He urged me one day to read Sidgwick, and I took his advice the next semester, with long-term consequences.

Most of my time was spent talking with Albritton and with Jerry Schaffer. They and a few other students had taken a seminar with J. O. Urmson, who'd been visiting the previous year. In it, they had been introduced to the latest Oxford style of analysis of ordinary language. Then, James Ward Smith, an assistant professor, returned from a stay in England with typescripts of Wittgenstein's still-unpublished "Blue and Brown Books." The department had copies made; we got them and did our best to absorb them. The senior faculty did not join in this endeavor. Their indifference added to our sense that we were engaged in a new and exciting venture, one that could change our whole discipline.

I could not, however, understand Sidgwick's *Methods of Ethics*. Albritton was not interested in him. And the faculty were no help. Sidgwick said he was trying to reconcile the utilitarians and the intuitionists. When I asked who the intuitionists were, Walter Stace replied: "Oh, you know, Moore and Prichard." Well, Sidgwick had taught Moore but was dead before Prichard published. There was very little secondary literature on Sidgwick, so I decided that I'd make him my dissertation topic. One trouble was that there was no one to direct it. In my third year, C. I. Lewis came as a visitor, and I was assigned to him. He, however, perhaps in Harvard style, never said anything about the quality of what I submitted to him. After I gave him a long chapter outlining and criticizing what I took to be Sidgwick's main argument, he said only: "Mr. Schneewind, don't you believe anything?" He left me with no idea of whether or not my work was acceptable. I learned only some years later that Lewis himself was then working out a view in ethics very much like the Sidgwickian line I had criticized.

In Murphy's graduate seminar on recent ethics, which I had taken as a senior, we read Toulmin's book on the place of reason in ethics. R. M. Hare's *The Language of Morals* was published the next year, in 1952. I found "analytic ethics" less interesting than I thought moral philosophy should be, and I was repelled by Hare's claim that ethics "is the logical study of the language of morals."[2] Surely there was more to it than that? Analytic ethics was not addressing the questions about morality and religion that I thought I would find help with. I turned back to John Stuart Mill to see if he agreed with Hare on what ethics was about. It seemed to me that Mill had far more substantial moral and political aims in mind. But I did not have time to follow up on this thought. My generous third-year fellowship was running out, and I had to find a job.

Morris Lazerowitz and Alice Ambrose invited me to come up to Smith College for an interview. A couple of weeks later, I got two job offers in the mail: one from Smith and one from the United States Army.

III

My two years in the army were spent mostly in Germany. I did clerical and administrative work, improved my German, evaded physical training, and traveled whenever I could. There was almost no philosophy in my life. Sidgwick was completely set aside. But I was bothered by Morris Lazerowitz's psychoanalytic interpretation of metaphysics, which he had explained to me at length during my visit to Smith. I kept thinking about the matter, so I covertly took time from my army clerical job to read McTaggart's *The Nature of Existence*, that most metaphysical of treatises. By the end of my military service, I was more or less ready to write a dissertation rebutting Lazerowitz and offering a new defense of metaphysics. Back at Princeton, John Yolton kindly agreed to read McTaggart and supervise my work. With his help and that of Gregory Vlastos, who had moved to Princeton, I was able to get a PhD by the end of my first year out of the army. In April of 1957, Warner Wick, who was visiting Princeton and along with me had been auditing Vlastos's seminar, offered me a job at the University of Chicago. In the autumn, I embarked on the grown-up part of a life full of philosophy.

At Chicago, the chairman allowed me to give a graduate seminar on Victorian moral philosophy. I began working seriously on Mill. Reading his early essays on "The Spirit of the Age," I saw that his moral thought was meant to respond to what he took as a need to rethink public morality in an age when religious certainties were fading. If he was interested in the logic of moral discourse, it was to aid his much larger project.[3] I wrote about this in introductions to two volumes reprinting Mill's shorter writings. Then, Paul Edwards asked me to write several articles on Victorians for his *Encyclopedia of Philosophy*, including a long one on Mill. I was also asked to write a book on the cultural and religious backgrounds of Victorian literature.

When I tried to understand Sidgwick the next time around, it was by taking a detour: finding out who those intuitionists were and what they were getting at. Chief among them was William Whewell. I'd found his major work in ethics by sheer chance, in a used-book store in New York, before I'd ever heard of him. Whewell was not an easy read, but his opposition to utilitarianism was evident. Sidgwick was widely supposed to be giving the finest account of classical utilitarianism. It baffled me to find that he himself insisted that he was not defending utilitarianism. He was just examining commonsense morality. Why was he doing that? Why did utilitarianism nonetheless matter so much to him?

What I discovered from my roundabout reading was that there were a number of Cambridge Anglicans—Whewell among them—who believed that evidence for God's existence could be found in the historical development of ordinary moral consciousness. That development, so they claimed, was a progressive revelation of God to mankind. Sidgwick had suffered a classic Victorian loss of his childhood religious faith. His examination of commonsense morality—so I thought—made sense as an effort to test this Anglican claim. Was the conventional morality of plain, unphilosophical people a site of progressive revelation? Was it coming ever closer to the ethics of Christianity?

The Cambridge Anglican claims about morality and revelation turned out to be the clue to Sidgwick's thought that I needed to get started on a book. Sidgwick's work, like Mill's, made much better sense to me when I could see how his arguments and positions were responding beyond philosophy to problems he saw in the culture of his own society. This insight, as I took it to be, shaped all the rest of my work. Like everyone else with an analytic background, I had had no training at all about how to work on the history of philosophy. Now I was learning that doing the history of moral philosophy required knowing a great deal about the philosophical, religious, and cultural contexts in which major works were written. Only so, I thought, could I grasp fully what the philosopher was doing, what were the problems he or she thought had to be addressed, and what lines of thought were or—more importantly—were not to be taken up and carried further. When I first met Quentin Skinner, many years later, I was already trying to understand the history of moral philosophy in ways similar to those he has so brilliantly defended for the history of political thought.

Mill's early work was not in print, so I was lucky that the libraries I could use enabled me to find it in the publications in which it first appeared. If I had not stumbled onto the Whewell book, I would have lacked an absolutely necessary resource for my Sidgwick work. It is a book that many libraries, even at good universities, do not have. Those were primitive days. There were no skateboards, no cell phones, and no Internet. There were also no modern editions of Hobbes or Locke or Hume. There were almost no reprints of minor writers, who were to be found only by hunting in used-book stores (I enjoyed that hunting to excess). The *Wellesley Index to Victorian Periodicals* had just come out. John Robson's great edition of John Stuart Mill had just been started. Machine-searchable and Web-based texts were not even dreamt of. One of the most significant changes in philosophical research in my lifetime has been the increase in the accessibility and accuracy of historical texts and commentaries on them. It has totally transformed historical research. The problem now is not mainly to get the material; it is what to do with so much of it.[4]

At Chicago, I had my first experience of job placement from the faculty side. In 1958, I was sent to the Western Division Meetings (as they were then called), carrying an armload of student folders and trailed by a flock of hopefuls. More often than not, they had just finished their master's degrees; only a few had begun doctoral dissertations. Those were the glory days when undergraduate enrollments were expanding rapidly and demand for teachers—any plausible teaching bodies—was high. The reception on the first evening was called "the smoker," and almost everyone smoked. Placement officers roamed the floor, buttonholing colleagues who were seeking new employees. Personal acquaintance was very important. Interviews were conducted on the spot or a day later. A good placement officer would be able to get a student five or six such contacts during the evening. That was the old-boy network.

It was fun working it all. But it seemed unfair to me. Those without well-connected protectors didn't have much of a chance. Albritton, Rawls, Malcolm, and some six or eight more of the well-connected at big universities began worrying about the unfairness of the procedure. Open advertisement of vacancies was the obvious solution, and some major departments agreed to advertise if the others would. Where could ads be published? I was deputed to check out costs at the *New York Times*. I quickly learned that the price per vacancy notice was prohibitively high. Moreover, most of the senior, well-connected professors liked the existing system and objected to changing it. What? Actually publish salaries? Give up our power over the young? Shocking!

It was only some years after our feeble first effort that the APA took on the task. The first issue of *Jobs in Philosophy* (as it was first called) came out in 1971.[5] It signaled a major change in the profession.[6]

IV

In 1960, for family reasons, I needed to be on the East Coast. Princeton kindly gave me a one-year position. Then, thanks to a paper on McTaggart, I was given a junior appointment at Yale, which later awarded me a third-year paid leave. One February morning in 1963, I asked John Smith, the department chair, if I would be reappointed afterwards. "No," he replied, "but you must remember that Yale is a good place to leave from." He was quite right. At noon the same day, I had lunch with Wilfrid Sellars, who offered me a tenured associate professorship at the University of Pittsburgh. I got married the next day, and in the autumn of 1964, after a leave, I began a happy decade in the growing Pitt department. Under the genial leadership of Kurt Baier, the department developed a stronger sense of common involvement in philosophy and in teaching than I've ever found anywhere else. Baier asked me to propose a program for majors. With much trepidation—recalling the rancor I'd seen at Yale—I presented a detailed plan. To my astonishment, everyone just agreed that we should adopt it. Of course, we had philosophical disagreements. But they never carried over into policy matters affecting everyone. Moreover, the department encouraged my research and waited patiently for a book on Sidgwick.

Meanwhile, civil rights movements and the Vietnam War were changing the atmosphere for moral and political philosophy. Analytic ethics was failing to interest undergraduates. Rawls's *A Theory of Justice* showed that philosophers could leave moral language aside and work again on more substantive issues. The development of what's called "applied ethics" began in the seventies. Philosophical discussions of the Vietnam War, and then of the oppression of black people and of women, further enriched the field. A. J. Ayer's *Language, Truth, and Logic* was one distinctive mark of a definite era in modern moral philosophy. John Rawls's *A Theory of Justice* initiated and deeply influenced another.[7] That shift was the most significant change in philosophical ethics that has occurred during my career.

I was already too deep into historical work for the new developments to redirect my research. But something altogether outside academe altered my life. In 1967–68, my family and I were in London where I was writing about Victorian thought. On April 4, 1968, Martin Luther King was assassinated. His death was the most important single event in shaping the place philosophy had in my life thereafter.

King's assassination made me ask myself if writing philosophy and its history was doing enough—was doing anything—to help with the social and political problems that were emerging in the turmoil at home. It seemed clear to me that it was not. I knew I had no gift for real-world politics. No matter what I might try, I would look and sound like a professor—not great for getting votes. I had no idea what I might do. But I felt ever more strongly that I ought not to remain just a passive observer.

Events provided me with what looked like an opportunity. Student protest movements continued in 1969. During the spring, Pitt undergraduates took over a new lecture hall built on a main street. I'd been departmental major advisor, and some of the student leaders were my advisees. The chancellor's deputy asked me to negotiate with them. After some difficulty, I got the administration to offer them the use of an older, less noticeable building for their headquarters and teach-ins. With more difficulty, I got the student leaders to accept the offer. Three days later, the chancellor asked me to become dean of the undergraduate college at Pitt. I had never considered administration, and I had no experience of it. Still, Pitt educated poor kids. Helping them get a good education would not alone solve America's major problems. But I thought it might be doing something for social justice, and in that naive belief, I accepted the position.

Much of my four-and-a-half years as dean was spent on efforts to change the curriculum and improve teaching. Cheered on by students, I led my faculty allies in battle against other faculty who I thought were impossibly conservative. We dropped the foreign-language requirement, opened the way to new multidisciplinary and "self-designed" majors, introduced new grading options, allowed students to vote on college policy matters, started having student evaluations of teaching—in short, carried out what was in fact the commonplace radical revisionism of the period. My partisans and I were sure our struggles were improving undergraduate education by giving the students far more freedom than they had ever had. A Hispanist political radical—Roberta Salper— whom I'd appointed assistant dean, asked me to help her start a women's studies program. Shaped as I was by John Stuart Mill's views on women, I agreed. We aroused much opposition, but we won. We created the first such program at a large public university, and it is still functioning. The nascent program in black studies similarly aroused much opposition, and I did what I could to help it survive. That program also lasted. Most of the other changes I convinced the college to adopt, however, disappeared to no one's regret under my successor. I consoled myself with the thought that at least I had made the faculty think anew about their teaching.

My own interest in teaching had begun in graduate school. Although I had a third-year fellowship, I wanted to teach, and I convinced the Princeton department to allow me to take a section in Walter Stace's big introductory course. When I asked to teach again in the spring, the chair decided that I ought to be paid. I think I was the first TA, at least the first paid TA, the Princeton department had ever had.

The job of undergraduate dean made me realize that my own teaching, though well-enough received, was quite conventional, and I tried to change it. More importantly, it made me aware that the APA itself had voiced no concern about teaching at all. In the early seventies, Maurice Mandelbaum, whom I'd met while I was at Yale, was chair of the APA Board of Officers. Despite his doubts about whether there was any need or any future for a committee on teaching, he gave me permission to form one on a temporary basis. Its innovative divisional programs were exceptionally well attended. After a year, the board conceded that the committee had some use, made it permanent, and appointed me its chair.

At the end of my term as dean, my family and I returned to England, where I finally started writing that book on Sidgwick. By the time we returned, I had nearly finished it. I let it be known that I was interested in administrative work at a school that aimed to educate poor city students. After some months, Jacqueline Wexler offered me the job of provost at Hunter College, CUNY. We moved to New York just as the city headed into a fiscal crisis. My first job as provost was to cut the faculty by 10 percent. Then finances got much worse. I set up a committee to steer us through the mess. We decided that we would have to cut whole departments and not rely on piecemeal attrition. It was impossibly difficult to decide which departments to close. At a climactic meeting, the committee told me that they had voted to have me alone make the final decisions. On the day I was to tell the president what I had decided, she informed me that the state was going to take over the whole of CUNY. We would not have to make the cuts. "So don't tell me what you decided," she said, "I never want to know." I never told her.

I lasted six years in the provost's job. During the first year, I finished the Sidgwick book. As I had done when I was a dean, I kept on teaching. While giving a graduate seminar in 1977, I came across Josef Schmucker's study of the development of Kant's ethics. It had not been reviewed in English. I thought perhaps I'd write a critical essay about it. What I wrote, instead, after many years, was *The Invention of Autonomy*.

As provost, I found what I had already experienced as a dean: that many faculty members are not only distrustful but disdainful of administrators. I recall visiting a Pitt historian and his wife one afternoon right after becoming dean and being dismayed when she asked whether we could still be friends. Most faculty members are quite incompetent about the practical affairs of a university, and most have absolutely no idea of the budgetary and political problems from which the administration shields them. Their uninformed contempt for administration unfortunately tends to steer away from it the few faculty members who might do it well.

Besides teaching and mulling over a Kant project, there were additional ways in which philosophy occupied much of my life while I was provost. I began to do a substantial amount of reviewing of grant and fellowship applications in philosophy. In 1977, I served for the first time on an external review committee for a philosophy department. In the next dozen or more years, I chaired or worked on over twenty such reviews. One of the visiting committees I chaired examined the Johns Hopkins department. Eventually, it accepted the committee's recommendation that it hire an outside person as chair. In 1980, I was offered the job. Jacqueline Wexler had left Hunter. Donna Shalala, the new president, was not comfortable with me nor I with her. In over ten years of administration, I had accomplished little more than helping to keep two worthy colleges going through difficult times, but I felt I could return to the professoriate without the uneasy conscience that had led me to move out of it. In 1981, I joined the Hopkins faculty.

V

We spent some twenty-three years in Baltimore. Managing the department was not onerous. The university was generous with time and money for research, and I obtained fellowship support as well. I wrote most of *The Invention of Autonomy* at the Center for Advanced Study in Stanford, a marvelous haven of assistance and intellectual camaraderie. I finished it with further assistance from Hopkins in 1996. But my administrative travails were not over.

In 1994, I was elected vice president of our division, and that, of course, led to the presidency for 1995–96. A few years later, I was astonished to be asked if I would stand for election to the chair of the National Board of the APA. I wanted to decline. I did not think I was of the philosophical eminence of those who had held the position previously. But knowledgeable friends, while not denying my point, said that the board at this juncture urgently needed someone with administrative experience. And the board chair had to be a past divisional president. I felt indebted to the APA, and I agreed to stand. I was elected to what turned out to be the most nerve-wracking position I've ever had.

In 1998, the most pressing problem for the national office was one of personnel. Philip Quinn, the then chair, told me that the members of the office staff were having trouble working together. The animosities were so great that it looked as if the collapse of the whole APA national operation was a real possibility. In cutting the budget at Hunter, I always worked as part of a large organization with many others sharing the burdens. I had no such support at the APA. A few of the divisional officers—particularly Bill Mann and Robin Smith—were helpful, and the staff who stayed after I made some personnel decisions were admirably loyal. But I felt that the burden of keeping the organization going was basically mine. I usually sleep soundly. I'd had one or two bad nights during the financial crises at Hunter College, but I lost much more sleep over the APA.

During the early stages of this tumultuous period, I frequently drove up to the national office at the University of Delaware in Newark to cope with the most urgent issues. Then I was lucky enough to get Richard Bett, a colleague of mine at Hopkins, to take over some of the responsibilities. His splendid performance relieved me of much work. Richard, however, did not want to continue on a regular basis. It was difficult to recruit someone for so unsettled an organization, but eventually, we found an excellent person to take the job, Elizabeth Radcliffe.[8] She ran the office very effectively for a year and a half, so I thought the worst of our problems were over. But then she decided to return to teaching. It was even harder this time around to find candidates for the position. Somehow, we managed, and when Judith Thomson took office as my successor, I thought I was handing her an organization that was at least in running order. I learned later that this had been a serious delusion on my part. By the time I found out, the APA was no longer my responsibility.

VI

Over the course of sixty years in philosophy, I've received much help from friends and colleagues. Richard Rorty was not only my closest friend, he was—after Kant—the most important influence on my thinking. We met in 1957. It was some years before we began discussing philosophy seriously, and when we did, I was already largely on his side. At Chicago and Yale, I'd taught Peirce and been convinced by his early anti-foundationalist arguments, and I'd published a paper arguing against foundationalism in ethics.[9] Rorty admired Dewey much more than I did and Peirce much less. We argued for more than forty years about what philosophy—particularly moral philosophy—might do and about the value of Kantianism. He frequently convinced me; I rarely managed to change his mind.[10] I think we both found our endless conversations edifying, as he would have said.

Mary Mothersill joined the Chicago philosophy department while I was there. In her uniquely droll and astringent way, she provided me with much-needed guidance as well as encouragement. It was from her that I first learned of the very hard time women encountered when trying to pursue a philosophical career. We kept in touch over the years, and she never stopped advising and encouraging me.

John Rawls introduced me to Derek Parfit at an APA meeting in the early seventies. When I was working on Sidgwick, Parfit's guidance was invaluable. He had already begun the thinking that led to his powerful *Reasons and Persons*, for which he'd found Sidgwick very stimulating. He opened my eyes to much about Sidgwick's arguments that would otherwise have escaped me altogether. Rawls himself was also a constant source of support in my historical endeavors. He was always my ideal reader. His approval of my two books was the best reward I could have gotten.

I have already mentioned the support and encouragement I received from the Pitt department. Once John Cooper joined it, he and I became close friends. For years now, I have relied on him for instruction and correction when I have rashly tried to write about ancient moral philosophy. Moreover, he took on the thankless task of being vice chair of the National Board of the APA. His shrewd and level-headed advice on APA matters was of inestimable value.

For about ten years at Johns Hopkins, I had the great benefit of the company of David Sachs. Upon learning that I'd read all of Pufendorf's massive treatise on the law of nature and of nations, he told me that I had a greater capacity for enduring boredom than anyone else he'd ever met. Nonetheless, he patiently read my drafts, always seeing what I was trying to do and unerringly pointing out where I was failing to do it. I have always regretted that he did not live to shred more of my early efforts to get straight about Kant and his predecessors.

Along with all this help, there were occasional personal discouragements. Warner Wick at Chicago said emphatically, in my hearing, that no one not raised as a Christian could really understand Christian thought. Derek Parfit relayed a remark by John Plamenatz, the Oxford historian of political philosophy, to whom he described my Sidgwick project. "No one can write such a book," Plamenatz said. Many years later, I was introduced to the distinguished German Kant scholar Konrad Cramer. On hearing my plans for a book on Kant and earlier moral philosophy, he replied instantly: "Aber Herr Schneewind, so einen Buch können Sie bestimmt nicht schreiben."[11]

Remarks like these helped teach me a lesson everyone should learn: that one often has to ignore advice from one's elders and betters. What mattered more to me than such personal road bumps was the general low esteem in which history of philosophy was held by philosophers. Quine thought historical work a waste of time for anyone seriously interested in philosophical problems. There were often-told tales of anti-history slogans on some office doors in major departments. The attitude was made vivid to me quite early in my career in a casual remark by William Frankena when I was talking with him at an APA meeting. I told him how much I admired his essays on the British moralists and reported that Dick Brandt thought he was going to expand them into a book. "Just like Brandt," Frankena snapped, "suggesting that I'm giving up philosophy and turning to history."

I was already sure that Frankena's disparaging contrast between doing philosophy and studying its history was misguided. I had no doubt that doing history of philosophy properly requires a philosophical understanding and assessment of what past thinkers have said. My own work on Mill and Sidgwick had convinced me that historical understanding was equally indispensable for any accurate reading of past philosophy. How could it be less so for our own? For a long time, I felt that my historical concerns alienated me from the main stream of English-language philosophy. But in recent years, antihistorical bias has noticeably decreased. A great deal of significant historical work has been published, including studies of neglected and "minor" past philosophers. More and more philosophers are realizing that their own work is as historically situated as that of the past major figures on whom we continue to comment. I take this to be at least the start of one more significant shift in professional philosophy, and I am happy to have made a small contribution to it.

I dedicate this lecture to the memory of Richard Rorty. "There is no action or thought in which I do not miss him, as indeed he would have missed me. For just as he surpassed me infinitely in every other ability and virtue, so he did in the duty of friendship."[12]

NOTES

John Dewey Lecture delivered before the 105th annual Eastern Division Meeting of the American Philosophical Association in Philadelphia, Pennsylvania, on December 29, 2008. Used by permission of the John Dewey Foundation.

1. Jerome Karabel, *The Chosen* (New York: Houghton Mifflin, 2005), 128. This important book is full of information on the history and practice of Jewish quotas. For a study of Yale and selective admission, particularly in the latter half of the twentieth century, see Joseph A. Soares, *The Power of Privilege* (Stanford, CA: Stanford University Press, 2007). Soares argues that although Yale's president Kingman Brewster dropped the Jewish quota, he continued

longstanding practices favoring a socioeconomic elite, disguised as meritocracy.

2. R. M. Hare, *The Language of Morals* (Oxford University Press, 1952), v.

3. See my introduction to *Mill's Ethical Writings* (New York: Collier Books, 1965), 13–17.

4. The increased ease of access to historical sources has been only a part of the massive growth in philosophical publication. It's hard to get accurate figures, but one well-informed estimate is that more than five thousand philosophy titles are published yearly. There are now over 150,000 philosophy books. Some five hundred journals are indexed annually in *Philosopher's Index*, which does not claim to cover everything. There are over 170 active philosophical societies in the United States alone. (I am indebted to George Leaman, director of the Philosophy Documentation Center, for these figures.)

All this is part of an overwhelming flood of new publications in general: Robert Darnton tells us that, in 2006, 291,920 new titles were published in the United States alone (*New York Review of Books*, June 12, 2008, 78). Internet publishing and reviewing are expanding so rapidly that any numbers I might report would be out of date. Myles Burnyeat writes of the 1960s as a time before philosophy "fell apart into specialisms." (See his introduction to *The Sense of the Past* by Bernard Williams, Princeton University Press, 2006, xiii.) Now we mostly ignore each others' areas: hard enough to keep up with one's own.

5. I am indebted to Janet Sample of the APA National Office for this and other information presented here.

6. I don't think the change was motivated solely, or even mainly, by mounting awareness of the unfairness of the old-boy system. The number of academics was growing rapidly all over the country, as was the number of colleges and universities. The old-boy system could not handle so many places and people. Consider only the numbers of registered philosophers: in 1948 the APA had just over one thousand members. Divisional meetings could be held on college campuses: I remember going to one at Yale in 1960. But that turned out to be the last Eastern Division Meeting held at a university. The next year we met in Atlantic City, and since then, it's been hotels in big cities every year. (The *Journal of Philosophy* used to print the programs and papers for the Eastern Division Meetings. It records the location of our meetings each year.)

By 1978, there were over five thousand APA members; now we have about thirteen thousand. Regular-session programs have gotten ever longer, and in 2007, more than eighty satellite organizations held their meetings when this division met. Little wonder that arranging meetings has become a major chore. (Thanks again to Janet Sample, and to Linda Smallbrook, for help here.)

In 1949, there were about 1,850 institutions of higher education in the United States. Fifty years later, there were over 4,000. Community colleges and, more recently, for-profit institutions multiplied and, with them, the numbers of faculty who had neither tenure nor prospects of getting it. In 1975, over 55 percent of faculty were either tenured or on tenure track. In 2005, only some 30 percent were in that happy position. (For data, see Jack H. Schuster and Martin J. Finkelstein, *The American Faculty* [Baltimore: Johns Hopkins University Press, 2006].) Professors at the elite universities mostly did not know those at less prestigious schools. As jobs became scarcer, however, it became increasingly important for even the top universities to be able to place their students outside the old charmed circles. Advertising became standard, as did arranging interviews through official placement services. Smoking ceased at the smokers—sorry, "receptions." If personal contacts didn't vanish so completely, they mattered much less. The numbers to be served, and an increasing concern about sexual harassment and gender and racial prejudice, forced everyone into the much more impersonal system we now have.

7. See my "Ethics: Hooker to Ayer" in *Continuum Encyclopedia of British Philosophy* (Bristol, UK: Thoemmes Continuum, 2006), 2:1014–22. I have discussed the impact on philosophical ethics of Rawls, the Vietnam War, and the civil rights movements of the seventies in "La philosophie morale au XXe siècle," in *Un siècle de philosophie 1900–2000* (Paris: Gallimard, 2000), 150–59.

8. Until we appointed Radcliffe, the chief administrative officer of the APA had received only a half-time salary from us. We depended on our host university to hire this officer for enough part-time teaching to make up a decent income. We learned that we could not attract anyone with that kind of arrangement. Consequently, we had to raise individual member dues and renegotiate the division of income received from book exhibits. It was not exactly easy to get the board and the divisions to go along with all this.

Other changes needed to be made as well—part of the growing pains due to the massive increase in the number of our members. We created the offices of vice chair and of treasurer and started the committee on diversity to represent all the increasingly numerous groups of philosophers who felt themselves to be outside the main stream of the profession. A fine report from a committee chaired by Karen Hanson helped us to make other significant changes in the way the board worked.

9. "Moral Knowledge and Moral Principles," delivered at the Royal Institute of Philosophy, London, November 1968; published in *Knowledge and Necessity*, ed. D. N. A. Vesey (London: MacMillan, 1970).

10. For a snapshot of our last conversations, see my essay on Rorty's ethics, and his reply, in the forthcoming Library of Living Philosophers volume on him.

11. "But Mr. Schneewind, you certainly can't write a book like that."

12. Montaigne, *Essays*, trans. Donald Frame (Stanford University Press, 1958), "Of Friendship," p. 143.

3

HOW IT WAS

Judith Jarvis Thomson

I

I had intended to take the premed program when I went to Barnard College in September 1946, but two things killed that idea in my first semester. First, you had to take a lot of chemistry, which required memorizing a lot of facts. Second, I had signed on for Introduction to Philosophy. I did so out of mere curiosity, since I had had no idea what philosophy was, and, lo and behold, met Berkeley's *Dialogues* there. It was certainly very obscure, but all the same, it was the most fascinating work I had ever read. Moreover, philosophy didn't require memorizing anything.

I think the philosophy program at Barnard was on the whole typical of those at other small four-year colleges in the late forties. What was called Modern Philosophy in course listings ended with Kant, though, if memory serves, you could do a reading course in post-Kantian philosophy through Hegel and the ethics course took us through Mill.

Barnard then had a distinguished philosopher visiting or on its faculty (I don't remember which): William Pepperell Montague. He was described to us as a New Realist, though I didn't then have (and still don't have) any clear idea what marked him off from the Objective Realists and the Critical Realists, who were also important figures in American philosophy at the time. I took either metaphysics or history of philosophy with him (I don't remember which) as a sophomore. I vaguely remember having found his course interesting, though the only thing I remember his telling us was that he didn't fancy kissing girls who wear lipstick because it would be like kissing buttered toast.

What I think was less adequate at Barnard than at other comparable colleges was its logic course. Our textbook was W. S. Jevons's *Elementary Lessons in Logic*, which was published in 1870. It was largely devoted to Aristotelian logic, with a couple of chapters on induction at the end. Aristotelian logic is a little more interesting than one might have thought, given the existence of procedures for reducing all valid syllogisms to the four valid syllogisms of the first figure. (The figure of a syllogism turns on the position of its middle term.) But only a little more interesting.

I should stress that it wasn't because Barnard was a women's college that its logic course was so thin. Barnard was a vigorously bluestocking enterprise and prided itself on the number of professional women among its graduates—as did Hunter College High School, which I had gone to before Barnard and which was then a girls' school. (Hunter later became coed.) So I am led to believe that the members of Barnard's philosophy department simply didn't think philosophy majors needed to be introduced to anything more sophisticated in logic than Jevons supplied us with. Whatever its source, I had cause to regret that gap in my background when I went to graduate school.

Meanwhile, it was my friends who introduced me to the twentieth century in philosophy—to works by G. E. Moore and A. J. Ayer in particular, and then to John Wisdom's dazzling papers on "Other Minds." It was the place of Cambridge in twentieth-century philosophy that led me to apply for a Fulbright scholarship to go to Cambridge rather than Oxford and Wisdom's papers that led me to apply to work with him there.

II

So I went to Cambridge. It was 1950, high noon of ordinary-language philosophy in England.

Some people use that term to refer to philosophy that (roughly) takes ordinary beliefs to constrain the acceptability of philosophical theories. On that construal of it, both Moore and Wittgenstein count as engaging in ordinary-language philosophy. Among the many reasons for welcoming Scott Soames's history of analytic philosophy is its distinguishing radically between the movement that Moore launched and the later movement that Wittgenstein launched.[1] According to Moore, the fact that ordinary beliefs are true is only the beginning of philosophy: the job of the right-thinking philosopher is then to analyze those beliefs—thereby solving the philosophical problems that philosophers have grieved over in the past. According to Wittgenstein, what were thought of as philosophical problems were just confusions about the workings of the relevant bits of language. So the job of the right-thinking philosopher isn't to solve problems, whether by analysis or anything else. His or her job is rather to bring out what the confusions are, thereby not solving, but dissolving, the (only putative) problems.

By 1950, it was the movement Wittgenstein had launched that dominated philosophy in England. His *Philosophical Investigations* wouldn't come out until 1953, but his influence was everywhere. Moreover, the "Blue and Brown Books" were circulating in typescript among the students. It was typical of the period, however, that the students who owned copies insisted that you get permission to read them from the appropriate authority else they wouldn't let you see theirs. The appropriate authority in Cambridge then was John Wisdom.

Cambridge was purer in its devotion to the leader than Oxford was. Oxford took pride in Gilbert Ryle's *The Concept of Mind*, which had been published in 1949, but it was full of philosophical theses that purported to be solutions to the (putative) problems about the mind that Wittgenstein had taught don't exist. Cambridge would have none of it—Cambridge didn't merely think Ryle's book wrong in letter, Cambridge thought it badly confused in spirit.

I think it a great pity that John Wisdom has disappeared from the history of the period—he doesn't even merit a footnote in Soames's history. Wisdom was always something of a cult figure, though he was much admired by the better-known philosophers of the period such as Austin, but he is no longer even a cult figure. I said earlier that his papers on "Other Minds" were dazzling—indeed, they are brilliant. There are eight papers in the series, and they appeared in issues of *Mind* from 1940 to 1943. Wisdom does in them exactly what Wittgenstein had said philosophers should do. He starts with the (so-called) other minds problem and then sails back and forth over all of the central areas of metaphysics, bringing out how we do and don't use the relevant bits of language, which bits are like which others, and what confuses us and why. I add that the papers are often witty, and they are rich in clever examples.

His lectures were like them. He was tall and bald and very thin, and his features were thin and sharp; he looked like a crow in the black MA gown that lecturers at Cambridge wore. At the first lecture that he gave that fall, he leaned on the lectern and rubbed his head and thought for a while, and then he finally asked us: "Was it negligence?" A story gradually emerged. Somebody (who?) had left a bucket at the head of the stairs (why?) and somebody else (who?) had tripped over the bucket (why?) and was hurt (how badly?) and so on. Wisdom brought out how the empirical and the a priori were tangled together in the enterprise of answering a question about what might have been an actual event.

Weekly supervision sessions with Wisdom took a lot of getting used to. At my first, he suggested that I give him something I had written as an undergraduate. "Well," he said at my second session, "I can see that you've read a lot of philosophy." Alas, there was no way in which that could be thought a compliment. My next assignment was to find a page or two, or perhaps a paragraph, of something by, as it might be, Russell and write a little paper on what goes on in it; then I was to read the paper to him at our next supervision session. Wisdom went on making similarly open-ended assignments, week after week. I add that his estimates of my work turned not only on what I wrote but also on whether the choice I had made of pages or paragraph was an interesting choice—I was to learn to tell the difference. That was unquestionably the best teaching that I had ever had.

I earlier described Cambridge as purer than Oxford, but it was of course only the part of Cambridge that I was fascinated by that I was referring to, the part led by Wittgenstein, with Wisdom as apostle-in-chief and Wisdom's students as disciples. Other things—some quite impure—also went on in Cambridge in successive terms in the two years I spent there. C. D. Broad and A. C. Ewing lectured on ethics; if memory serves, G. H. von Wright lectured on deontic logic and R. B. Braithwaite on philosophy of science. Peter Geach gave some lectures on Frege; I greatly regret that I didn't come to see the importance of the issues that Geach lectured on then until many years later. Moore and Wittgenstein were still alive while I was there but did no lecturing that I was aware of.

III

Wonderful as it all seemed, I was in fact reading less and less philosophy as time passed and taking it less and less seriously. Not surprisingly, I didn't do well on my final exams, and I concluded that I wasn't really any good at philosophy. Moreover, the subject didn't seem as exciting as it had when I first arrived in Cambridge. Berkeley's *Dialogues* now seemed less interesting than they had when I was an undergraduate since I had by now learned that there wasn't any real problem that Berkeley was trying to solve and that what was to be done with his text was just to work out what mistakes about the relevant bits of language were responsible for its obscurity.

So I quit. There was no disloyalty to anything or anyone in doing so since Wittgenstein himself took the view that we should all quit.

I tried advertising when I got home to New York. I began with a job as a copywriting trainee at J. Walter Thompson—I became fairly good at writing ads for My-T-Fine Chocolate Pudding and Fleischmann's Active Dry Yeast. But only fairly good, not very good, because writing lively ads turned out to require a talent I discovered that I didn't have. (Academics harbor the idea that they could conquer the business world and make fortunes if their love of their subjects didn't keep them poor in academe. For most of us, nothing could be further from the truth.)

After drifting to other advertising jobs, I met a man at a party who was in search of a ghost. He was full of ideas about how to overhaul the American public-school system, but they were a great clutter, and he thought he needed someone to organize them into a book for him. That, anyway, seemed to me to be something I could do reasonably well and would certainly prefer to advertising, so I signed on for a trial run.

Ghosting isn't a nine-to-five job: you can do it as well at midnight as at noon. So I thought I would sit in on a midday philosophy course at Columbia just to see how philosophy sounded after my something over two years since Cambridge.

IV

It sounded terrific. I had had the great good luck to opt to sit in on John Herman Randall's yearlong course on the history of philosophy. It made

me finally take seriously something that had all along been obvious
enough: if philosophers' worries all issue just from their misuse of the
relevant bits of language, then it would be amazing that the bits of
language misused by those of one generation, who wrote in one language, just happen to be roughly translatable into the bits of language
misused by those of a different generation, who wrote in a different
language. (In English: matter, time, space, cause, person, mind, knowledge, good, and so on.) No doubt there were several possible ways of
explaining those similarities among philosophers. I took them to suggest, and finally to show, that philosophers across time and language are
engaged in a common enterprise—that they are trying to solve the same
problems and facing the same difficulties in solving them. I am sure
that that wasn't what Randall intended us to conclude. Similarities
among philosophers of course mattered to him, but what he again and
again drew our attention to were differences, among others, the differences due to advances in science. I didn't care about the differences.
What mattered to me was the shared problems—and it didn't take long
before I realized that nothing interested me anywhere near as much as
they did.

So I thought I would have another go at philosophy: I applied for a
place as a regular graduate student at Columbia. I can't think why the
department accepted me as a full-time student, given my lack of success
at Cambridge, but incredibly, they did. So I ceased being a ghost and
came back to life.

V

It was then that I first met active, as opposed to history-book, discrimination against women. I hadn't met any at Hunter or Barnard, of
course, and I hadn't really had cause to notice any at Cambridge. (The
English seem to have been far more relaxed about the presence of
women in universities than Americans were.) The then chairman of the
Columbia philosophy department said when I applied for admission
that he hoped I would enjoy doing philosophy for its own sake because I
mustn't suppose I could ever get a job as a teacher of philosophy. He
said that philosophy departments don't hire women except as secretar-
ies, and a fortiori, that Columbia wouldn't support my candidacy for a

teaching job. Many women have described the insults they had to become accustomed to in academe; mine were like them. I mention only how long even the most overt discrimination lasted. I had occasion to need a temporary job in the Boston area in the mid-sixties, some years after I had received my PhD, and I had asked a friend of my husband's and mine who was then a member of the Harvard philosophy department whether he thought I could get some TA-ing to do for his department. Our friend said no—his department wouldn't entrust its undergraduates to women, even as TAs.

VI

Still, it was delightful to be a graduate student again in the mid-fifties.

Columbia's philosophy department was largely divided between those who worked in the history of philosophy and those who worked primarily with Ernest Nagel in the philosophy of science. (The New, Objective, and Critical Realists had disappeared by then.) I plainly wasn't going to concentrate anywhere in the history of philosophy, and though I took all the courses that Nagel offered, and he would later agree to chair my dissertation committee, I equally plainly wasn't going to concentrate anywhere in the philosophy of science. (For better in some ways and worse in others, I remained a former student of John Wisdom's.) What was so delightful about being at Columbia then, and what I learned most from, was the informal talk—with my contemporaries, Arthur Collins and a graduate student from Greece, Costas Politis, and with two of the junior faculty members, Arthur Danto and Sidney Morgenbesser.

An even greater piece of good luck for me came when the chairman of the philosophy department at Barnard, Joe Brennan, offered me a teaching job there. The chairman of the Columbia philosophy department had evidently forgotten about the existence of women's colleges, even the one right across the street, and a fortiori had forgotten that women's colleges made serious efforts to see to it that women were well represented on their faculties. (Many women of my generation, in many fields, had good reason to be grateful to the women's colleges.) The older members of Barnard's department, who had been my teachers only a few years ago, had by now retired or died, and the chairman was in process of rebuilding.

VII

Nothing could have been happier. I hadn't realized how much I would enjoy teaching philosophy. That I did was partly due to the fact that my students at Barnard were smart and enthusiastic. It was also due to the fact that teaching required taking stands on philosophical issues, or justifying one's inability to take them, and then defending oneself against objections from students—discussion and argument, week after week, all term long. I loved it.

A way of understanding what philosophy is came to seem to me increasingly plausible. I had already come to think that philosophy consists in a battery of problems; back at Barnard again, I came to think that the main, central problems consist in efforts to explain what makes certain pre-philosophical, or nonphilosophical, beliefs true. Which beliefs? Philosophers differ in their interests, but the ones that have interested philosophers, generally, in generation after generation, are those that we rely on in ordinary life. Not surprisingly, it was Moore, not Wittgenstein, who struck me as the leader. (I suspect that I could have said Aristotle instead of Moore.) I still think that way of understanding what philosophy is is roughly right.

VIII

But only roughly, since so much in it is unclear. For example, which nonphilosophical beliefs are such that a philosopher tries to explain what makes them true? Moore had invited us to take the beliefs to include that there are living human bodies, which have been in contact with or near the surface of the earth since they were born, that some events had occurred before others, and that there are human beings like oneself in having experiences. But that is an awfully short list. For one among many examples of missing kinds of proposition, there is nothing normative on the list, and, in particular, no moral directives to the effect that such and such a person ought or ought not do such and such.

I hadn't been interested in ethics until I started teaching, except as a minor branch of metaphysics. But I had to become interested in it, and quickly at that, because as the junior member of the Barnard department, I had to teach the 9 a.m. class on Monday, Wednesday, and Friday, which happened to be Introduction to Philosophy. It was then that I began to wonder why there weren't any moral directives on Moore's list. It seemed to me clear that there are moral directives that are as obviously true as that there are a lot of living human bodies currently near the surface of the earth.

I was pleased to find that question about Moore's list in Soames's history because my first published paper (in 1958) was an effort to show that some moral directives do belong on Moore's list. Unfortunately, while I still think the question first-rate, my effort to answer it then was really pretty bad.

Mainstream ethics in the late fifties was wholly metaethics. For example, Hare's *The Language of Morals* had come out in 1952, and that and other efforts to accommodate expressivism in some way, or to rebut it, were widely discussed.

Ten years later, mainstream ethics began to look very different: there was a dramatic turn in what could be done by academic philosophers under the name "ethics." The turn was due to the Vietnam War, which affected campuses across the country. Many moral philosophers came to believe that they had been at fault for failing to take concrete moral issues generally as seriously as they should have. Philosophers interested in ethics began publishing papers on topics that the standard philosophy journals had never published papers on before—we wrote on topics such as abortion, just war, the right to privacy, self-defense, and affirmative action and preferential hiring and the rights of women and minorities more generally. It was remarkable! Much of that material was at first published in *Philosophy and Public Affairs*, which was founded by Marshall Cohen in 1971: it invited lawyers and political theorists to join moral philosophers in dealing with concrete moral issues and was an immediate success.

My impression is that by the mid-eighties that enthusiasm for attending to concrete moral issues had begun to abate. Such material continues to be published, of course, in many other journals as well as in *Philosophy and Public Affairs*. But my impression is that the new moves that were being made in ethics by the mid-eighties were largely moves in metaethics. I had myself begun to find legal theory and the theory of rights of particular interest.

IX

By that time, I had married an English philosopher, James Thomson, and we had moved to Boston and to positions at MIT. MIT had decided to develop a graduate program in philosophy in the early sixties—funds were available, and expansion was common in many fields in universities across the country. James was invited to join in 1964, and when MIT discovered that what it had described to us as a nepotism rule was really only a nepotism policy, I was allowed to join in 1965. (MIT quietly shelved that policy in the coming years.)

The new philosophy graduate program was to fit its surroundings at MIT: it was to have philosophy of language, logic, and science at its heart. That is what had attracted James from the outset. I came to realize its advantages for me only gradually, but it didn't take very long for them to become clear. My interests had been divided between metaphysics and ethics during my years at Barnard, and they continued to be divided in that way at MIT. My work in both areas greatly benefitted from discussion with James and with those who joined the program as the years passed—I thank the graduate students as well as the faculty members that MIT has been lucky enough to attract.

X

Many philosophers say these days that nothing new has happened in philosophy in recent years and that philosophers are just marking time. I would be clearer about whether to agree if I were clearer about what they take to be missing.

My impression is that the major moves in philosophy have always issued from the development of a new meta-philosophy. The great figures of the past, such as Aristotle, Descartes, Hume, and Kant, didn't just produce new theories in one or other of the subfields of philosophy, such as metaphysics or epistemology or ethics. They produced new ways of doing philosophy, the use of which yielded, or anyway created space for, new theories in several subfields. And it might be that there won't be any more such moves. Philosophers specialize nowadays. Hardly anyone is really at home in philosophy across the subfields—keeping up with developments in one subfield is just about a full-time job. It is arguable that that isn't due, or anyway isn't wholly due, to the fact that so much progress is currently being made in the individual subfields. Progress certainly has been and is being made in the subfields, but it is arguable that the specialization is at least in part due to the explosion of publication in philosophy due to the fact that publication is nowadays not only required for getting tenure, but advisable for getting a tenure-track job to begin with. Demand then generates supply, and journals proliferate.

Whether or not it is right to think that there won't be any more major moves in philosophy, that is, any more large-scale cross-subfield moves, there will surely be more moves within the subfields. The moves within subfields are most often made by a philosopher who finds an interesting new problem. Perhaps a philosopher draws attention to something that hadn't been noticed or had been noticed but hadn't been taken seriously before, as, for example, Goodman did when he drew attention to the fact that the data that support the claim that all emeralds are green are translatable into data that equally support the claim that all emeralds are grue. Or as Williams and Nagel did when they drew attention to moral luck. A great many moves of this relatively narrow kind were made in the last century, and many of them are lovely—not merely in themselves, but also in the fact that attention to them brings out the need for new theories.

Second, less common, are the new theories themselves—for example, Rawls's theory of justice, and Stalnaker's and Lewis's analyses of counterfactuals.

It is largely works of those two *intra*-specialty kinds—the new problems and the new theories—and the literature they generate, that fill all those journals. I don't see any good reason to think that the sources of works of such kinds are drying up. Thus, it seems to me that but for the shortage of jobs in philosophy that generated that explosion of publication, the condition of philosophy nowadays is pretty good.

Nevertheless, it is a pity that something more general is missing. I am going to take the liberty of describing something I would like to see done.

XI

Let us go back to Moore's list. I mentioned that moral directives—among propositions of many other kinds—are missing.

Here is an example that is familiar from the literature: we ought not kill one person to save five. Or a bit more careful: we ought not kill one bystander even if we would thereby save the lives of five bystanders from being killed by someone else. *I* think that belongs on Moore's list because I think it obviously true.

I will call those of us who think it obviously true the Believers. There are philosophers who think the Believers mistaken. On their view, if we are so situated, then we ought to kill the one bystander. Those philosophers are of course the Consequentialists.

The interesting fact isn't just that Consequentialists disagree; it is that they have a reason for disagreeing, a reason of an important kind: they have a plausible theory that yields that we ought to kill the one bystander and, indeed, explains why we ought to. Their theory says that what a person ought to do is what would maximize goodness. And they add that, other things being equal, we would in fact maximize goodness if we killed the one bystander, for four fewer will be killed if we do than if we don't.

The Believers, of course, think that the Consequentialists' theory not only isn't plausible but is false. But they have no plausible theory that yields that we ought not kill the one bystander and explains why we ought not. The literature contains lots of efforts, none convincing. The Consequentialists take considerable comfort in that fact. They say that the Believers' lack of a plausible theory shows that their belief is a mere intuition, which may be just a residue of "arbitrary and obsolete tradition."[2]

The fact that the Believers have no theory that would explain what they take to be a moral fact really does seem to weaken their case against Consequentialism. And isn't it right that it should? Eddington said somewhere that we should never trust the result of an experiment unless we have a theory that would explain it. A very attractive principle!

Eddington was talking about the sciences, of course, and not about philosophy, and there is a substantial literature on the role that scientific theories play in our understanding of the world around us. Philosophy is an armchair enterprise, and the role that philosophical theories play in our understanding of the world around us is arguably very different from that which scientific theories play. It is certainly plausible that philosophical theories play *an* important role in our understanding of the world around us, and it would be very welcome to hear about how they do from some contemporary philosophers. Why, after all, do we all work so hard at trying to solve philosophical problems and construct philosophical theories? (Why didn't we become physicists or anthropologists?)

I add that answering that question is the more difficult when we remember that the availability of a philosophical theory doesn't always play the evidential role that Consequentialism seems to play. Timothy Williamson recently drew attention to the fact that Gettier overturned the then most popular theory of knowledge overnight.[3]

According to that theory, for a person to know that p is for the person to have a justified true belief that p. What could be more plausible? Here is an example of the kind of case Gettier drew attention to. Alfred sends us excellent faked evidence that he is now in Paris. We therefore believe he is in Paris. We therefore conclude that he is in Europe. He is in Europe, but in Rome, not Paris. So while our belief that Alfred is in Europe is a justified true belief, we don't know that he is in Europe. Just about everyone agreed that Gettier had thereby refuted the justified true belief theory of knowledge. Nobody then had, indeed nobody now has, a more plausible theory of knowledge. Yet *nobody* said, "Listen Gettier, your lack of a plausible theory of knowledge shows that your belief that we don't know that Alfred is in Europe is a mere intuition, which may be just a residue of an arbitrary and obsolete tradition."[4] Why did Gettier come off so much better in his attempt at refuting the justified true belief theory of knowledge than we Believers come off in our attempt at refuting Consequentialism?

Is that difference due to the fact that Consequentialism is a normative theory whereas the justified true belief theory of knowledge is not? And thus that some version of expressivism must be right? I doubt it.

Producing a putative counter-case certainly doesn't always refute a plausible nonnormative philosophical theory. So why some theories and not others?

In sum, there are two questions I would welcome seeing work on. First, there is the question why we care about philosophical theories—what have we got when we've got one? And connected, second, why do some philosophical theories seem safer against counter-cases than others do? (I doubt that the first question can be answered without answering the second.) Both of the questions are meta-philosophical. Encouraged by Williamson and others, there is already the beginnings of a contemporary literature on meta-philosophy, and I greatly hope there will be more. I also hope that some Believer will be able to produce a plausible theory that yields that, and explains why, we must not kill that one bystander, and I also hope that some epistemologist will be able to produce an acceptable theory of knowledge. There is no incompatibility in hoping for good philosophy as well as for good meta-philosophy. But I think it pays to stress the value of meta-philosophy nowadays since we seem to have lost sight of it. There is certainly room for progress to be made on it even if we aren't going to be lucky enough to be granted another Aristotle, Descartes, Hume, or Kant.

NOTES

John Dewey Lecture delivered before the 109th annual Eastern Division Meeting of the American Philosophical Association in Atlanta, Georgia, on December 29, 2012. Used by permission of the John Dewey Foundation.

1. Scott Soames, *Philosophical Analysis in the Twentieth Century*, 2 vols. (Princeton, NJ: Princeton University Press, 2003).

2. Alan Strudler and David Wasserman, "The First Dogma of Deontology: The Doctrine of Doing and Allowing and the Notion of a Say," *Philosophical Studies* 80 (1995): 51.

3. Timothy Williamson, *The Philosophy of Philosophy* (New York: Wiley-Blackwell, 2007).

4. Well, hardly anybody. I thank Richard Holton for drawing my attention after the APA session to Brian Weatherson's saying something very like it in "What Good Are Counterexamples?" in *Philosophical Studies* 115 (2003): 1–31. I thank him for drawing my attention also to Jennifer Nagel's "Epistemic Intuitions," *Philosophy Compass* 2, no. 6 (2007): 792–819, which contains a

survey of the different positions that epistemologists have taken in recent years about epistemic intuitions and their relations to epistemic theories.

4

A PHILOSOPHER'S CALLING

Ruth Barcan Marcus

By age three, I had somehow taught myself to read by mimicking my older sisters. I recall reading about Chicken Little with the book turned upside down. But then one day, the sky was falling right side up. I was reading. It just happened. I also loved numbers and had some computational skills, which were willingly demonstrated. I also had eidetic memory. Some of those abilities gradually faded.

I grew up in a socialist household in the upper reaches of New York City. Our neighborhood was ethnically and religiously mixed but white and sparsely populated. Over the years, it became more densely populated as apartment buildings devoured the lots on which we played. There was a vast neo-Gothic Catholic church at the base of the hill where we lived and a Swedish Lutheran church facing us. The Lutheran church displayed a triangle on which was inscribed, "Seek and ye shall find God is Love." It eluded my understanding. On Sundays, there was an influx of worshipers from other parts of the city.

Our sainted figure was Eugene Victor Debs. A bronze bust of Debs graced our living room. The un-pictured arch villain was Joseph Stalin. My father's brother remained in what became the Soviet Union and then disappeared, presumably in Stalin's purge. I recall being at a fundraiser with my father in Madison Square Garden. It was for Norman Thomas, the socialist presidential candidate. Pledges came audibly from the audience, and my comment was that Anonymous must be very rich.

At that time, socialists and communists were enemies who inhabited parallel universes. They both sang variants of "The International" and carried red flags in May Day parades along different routes laid out by New York's finest. "They" had Young Pioneer and Young Communist League youth groups; "we" had the Red Falcons and the Young People's Socialist League. Which brings me to my first exposure to philosophy: in this case, political philosophy. Red Falcons had various programs, one of which was instruction in Marxist theory. Marx for tots. I recall being told about the theory of surplus value. An example, presented with illustrations, was a sweatshop where men's trousers were manufactured. Excess inventory accumulated and could not be sold. Workers were made redundant. A depression followed. It was all quite theoretical. The actual depression which we endured came later, but I recall that even at eight (or nine) a causal explanation for a historical event supported by putative arguments and evidence impressed me. Many Marxist slogans, such as "Each should produce according to his abilities and receive according to his needs," seemed to me fair, but I noted that it didn't fit observed practice. This set me to explicit thinking about fairness and justice. That particular slogan was more recently echoed in discussions of moral luck.

Nineteen thirty was a catastrophic year. My father died, and the Great Depression descended. My mother mourned all her life. We were now a family of four females, which I mention because I believe I had an easier time following an unconventional path than if there had been a strong male presence in the family.

The grade school I attended was confining, rigid, and above all boring. My education was extracurricular. I was a voracious reader, and the local library was accommodating. Afternoons, there was also some informal, nonprofit schooling, and, weather permitting, there were street games and excursions to local parks. Stickball was the staple. Also red rover, leapfrog, and variations of tag, along with quieter pursuits such as hopscotch, marbles, card games, etc. Girls at that time did not wear trousers. Sometimes my skirts flew, and neighbors complained at what seemed to them unseemly behavior but with little effect. Then, when I was of middle-school age, there was a welcome change in my schooling. It was called "progressive education" and was a consequence, I learned much later, of John Dewey's views on proper educational practice. He urged abandonment of the rigid formalities of traditional education. Learning is doing!

A new experimental junior-high school was designed for talented students and privately funded by the Ridder family. Admission was to be determined by test and by conferences with teachers, parents, and the candidate for admission. The tests marked me for admission, but I was seen as a "behavior problem," and there was much hesitation as to my admissibility. I had learned enough about plans for the school to realize that it would release me from the bondage of sitting rigidly behind a desk fixed to the floor, forbidden to talk with neighbors, and bored out of my skull. I even improvised a prayer to be admitted, and it was answered. I was admitted, and my expectations were not disappointed. Liberated at last, I was overcome with a desire to learn. Omniscience beckoned. I took to academic work with focus and unbounded enthusiasm. There is not the time to describe my many enthusiasms, but I must mention Euclidean geometry and the concept of rigorous proof.

Two years in junior high, three years in high school, and I was ready for college. At that time, it was expected that high-achieving girls from the city would attend Hunter College. Many of them would then make up a pool of prospective teachers for New York City schools. I had no clear future plans but nonetheless saw that Hunter College was too structured, stifling with uninteresting requirements, and altogether unappealing. It was also single sex. So, after a few days at Hunter, I took myself to Washington Square College of NYU. I enrolled, helped by some NY State Regent scholarships and the New Deal's funding of student jobs—I assisted the fencing coach at fifty cents per hour. There may have been other sources of financial support which I no longer remember.

Greenwich Village was a ferment. The philosophy department was in a building which abutted the location of the infamous Triangle Shirtwaist Factory Fire. The college lounges and cafeteria, the local restaurants and bars, and Washington Square itself were hosts to writers, entertainers, jazz buffs, *Partisan Review* hangers-on, and all manner of political—non-Stalinist—splinter groups (e.g., Musteites, Trotskyites, Lovestoneites, Schactmanites, the Socialist Workers Party, the Workers Party, and others). But the excitement did not distract me from the determination to seek a classical education: mathematics, physics, classics, history, and, of course, philosophy. Since I was an obsessive reader of fiction and criticism, both literary and social, and since a course entitled A Survey of English Literature was a disappointment, literature courses were thereafter excluded from the grand plan but continued to be part of my extracurricular self-education. My dual major was mathematics and philosophy.

The chair of the NYU philosophy department was Sidney Hook, one of the former Marxists whose God had failed. He was now a Deweyan pragmatist, and pragmatism dominated the department. Hook was a persuasive lecturer. Under his tutelage, the scientific method was now advanced above all others in the pursuit of knowledge. Dialectical materialism had long since been abandoned. His celebrated course was Philosophy of History and Civilization, a subject which has waned. The steps of the experimental (or scientific) method, proceeding from doubt to warranted assertability, were often intoned like a mantra. It was to me a plausible epistemological view. In the department, pragmatism thrived in harmony with logical positivism and its variants, logical empiricism and scientific empiricism. But the positivists, unlike the pragmatists, did not frown on the pursuit of truth or certainty. (Carnap said of philosophy that it is "the logic of science, i.e., the logical analysis of the concepts, propositions, proofs, theories of science,"[1] which meshed well enough with Dewey's pragmatism.) Pragmatists and positivists were later amply represented in the *Encyclopedia of Unified Science* side by side.

My original focus was not to take or defend this or that view. I wanted to understand the important philosophical texts of Plato, Aristotle, the empiricists, Kant, etc. There were courses in the history of ancient, medieval, and modern philosophy. Such study was a facet of my interest in the history of ideas, which was fired in part by an extracurricular reading of Arthur Lovejoy's *Great Chain of Being*.[2] The metaphysical notion of Being was a notion that would not survive for me as empirically meaningful. Fully meaningful or not, it continued to play a vital role in the history of metaphysics. The continuing appeal of such deeply obscure (at least to me) notions was baffling. Similarly, big questions like "Why is there something rather than nothing?" or "What is the meaning of life?" baffled me. I was hard put to understand what was being asked.

It wasn't philosophical accounts of meaning which led me to question the sense of such queries. It was my ordinary understanding via my ordinary language and my ordinary, commonsense experience. This is usually where I begin my philosophical inquiries. Austin and "ordinary-language philosophy" had, and continue to have, a strong appeal.

I have a long memory for popular tunes and lyrics, and it was long before my exposure to theories of meaning when I tried to fathom what was being asked by a popular ballad:

"Why was I born? Why am I living? What do I get? What am I giving?"

What would count as an answer? But, as in the case of my study of literature, my study of those philosophers whom I found deeply interesting but often irrational or obscure (for example, Nietzsche and Schopenhauer) was also extracurricular. I read the texts but took no courses.

At that time, the 1930s, philosophy was of widespread interest, especially political philosophy. At NYU, there was a philosophy club, over which I presided, with a university-wide membership, invited speakers, and heated debate. I recall an occasion when Mortimer Adler spoke and was relentlessly harangued. Hook suggested that, as president, I write an apology.

Interest in philosophy has gradually diminished and will, I believe, continue to wane, or at least its contours will change. Widespread interest among students has declined. There are, to be sure, as there always have been, spin-offs or quasi-spin-offs—for example, experimental philosophy, cognitive science, neuroethics, bioethics, feminist and transgender philosophy, black philosophy, and so on—but many of the spin-offs do not have settled constituencies. There has also been a revival of interest in traditional metaphysics among some analytic philosophers, partially fueled by an interest in modalities, but philosophy no longer has the widespread undergraduate appeal it once had.

Returning now to NYU's philosophy faculty, there were some who were especially memorable to me but probably unknown to most or all of you. I'll mention two: James Burnham and Albert Hofstadter. Burnham, who with Philip Wheelwright had written a good introductory text, *Introduction to Philosophical Analysis*,[3] was a teacher of extraordinary sensibility, who taught inter alia Aquinas and Dante, Thought and Literature of the Renaissance, and aesthetics. We gained some insight into the medieval and Renaissance world views; we learned how to look at pictures and how to read poetry. When he read to us, it was revelatory. I especially recall his mellifluous readings from Dante and Chaucer. Burnham was an American aristocrat who became a political activist turned Trotskyite after other, radical affiliations. When the German-American Bund goose-stepped its way into Madison Square Garden during the time of the Russian German Pact, we went to protest. Communists were conspicuously absent. Burnham, noticeably styled by Princeton and Oxford, confronted the mounted police—a memorable encounter. But not long thereafter, he returned to his conservative roots. He wrote *The Managerial Revolution*,[4] and *The Machiavellians*,[5] withdrew from academic philosophy, and became a political commentator for *National Review*. Go figure.

There was also Albert Hofstadter, who had collaborated with J. C. C. McKinsey of the mathematics department on a paper on the logic of imperatives.[6] It was a time when ethics was viewed by some to be grounded in a system of moral imperatives. The paper was an instructive example of how formal methods might be applied to some noncognitive theories. But then, Hofstadter too drifted away from logical empiricism. En route, he introduced us to Bradley and Bosanquet: my first encounter with Anglo-idealism. Hofstadter, like other faculty whom I admired, was interested in understanding philosophical issues or themes as they evolved over time. They shared the intensity of those interests with their students. Studying philosophy wasn't just an intellectual exercise or an assimilation of texts.

I was also a mathematics major, and, after two logic courses, J. C. C. McKinsey sponsored me for membership in an honors seminar in the mathematics department. At the time, there were no suitable texts in English devised for the advanced study of mathematical logic. McKinsey would select a suitable treatise or monograph which could be used. We started with one by D. Hilbert and P. Bernays, *Grundlagen der Mathematik*,[7] which McKinsey translated from the German. He wrote the translation on lined yellow pads and devised exercises. We met once or twice a week for as much as three hours in Bickford's cafeteria, a mainstay of the Village. The fruits of our study were presented to the mathematics honors seminar. It did not occur to me that the attention I received was special, which of course it was. It was, I thought, what college professors did routinely.

I had along the way become interested in C. I. Lewis and modalities, which McKinsey encouraged. Tarski was stranded in New York City at the time, and he and McKinsey collaborated on a study of modal and intuitionistic logic. I worked on proving completeness for Lewis's favorite system, S3, and did not succeed but was not discouraged.

Professors McKinsey and Hook urged me to go on to graduate work. Time and again my mother expressed uneasiness, which was echoed by others: was it a suitable career? I was eighteen and, as before, wasn't thinking about a career or profession. It was an interest infused with passion. I was advised *not* to apply to Harvard given my interest in modal logic, upon which W. V. Quine, the dominant presence at Harvard, cast a very cold eye. I was advised to apply to Yale, where Professor F. B. Fitch would be more sympathetic. So I applied and was admitted to Yale.

My initial impression of Yale upon arriving in New Haven in 1941 was of a romantic, Gothic fantasy of a university. Despite the difficulties I encountered, the joy at being there was sustained. I sometimes stayed on during breaks so I could inhabit the library, wander about, and pretend possession. But there were problems. (Our "problems" are today's "issues.") Housing for women was separate but not equal. It came with house rules, a curfew, and a housemother. I sought digs elsewhere, where my nocturnal habits were tolerated. We did share a dining room with men, but few women were visible.

In a report in the Yale archives, the graduate dean is reported as saying, "Yale had admitted women to its Graduate School as early as 1892 but had made no provision for their needs as human beings." He also notes,

> My suggestion in 1942 that Yale commemorate in some simple fashion her half century of higher education for women was rejected with scorn by the Secretary of the university who was the panjandrum of official ceremonies. His attitude was typical of older Yale College graduates in the faculty and administration. They appeared to be embarrassed by the presence of women in the student body and would have no part in calling attention to Yale's lapse in the matter.[8]

Women were unwelcome in the room of the library where contemporary fiction and criticism were shelved. It was furnished like a comfortable men's club. I protested, and a compromise was reached. Books women wanted would be passed out to be read elsewhere. Also, women could not enter undergraduate classrooms even where they were assisting with grading. There were recurrent discriminatory episodes. I'll mention one graphic incident among many. Yale had a philosophy club open to undergraduate and graduate students. I was elected president but then received a letter from the chair of the department suggesting that I decline. The reasons given were that Yale was predominantly and historically a male institution and that my election may have been a courtesy. Also, the club's executive committee met at Mory's, which was closed to women. I did not respond to the letter and did not decline. It was, to me, obviously unreasonable. When the letter was discussed in the graduate dining room, several students said it was imprudent to have revealed it since the chair influences job placement. My response was as before: I wasn't thinking about a job. I assumed the presidency, and the executive committee did not meet at Mory's (which was not "liberated" until the seventies).

My work in the department was satisfying. Especially logic with Fitch; Leibniz and Kant's critiques with Ernst Cassirer; philosophy of science with Cassirer, Northrup, and Margenau (of the physics department); and wonderful discussions with Charles Stevenson and Monroe Beardsley. Cassirer was a stellar teacher and a polymath who could convert positivists into Kantian idealists.

I had a copy of the second edition of *Principia Mathematica*, which was purchased out of a $100 book prize awarded to a first-year student and which I began to study systematically. I then went on to study Russell's *Principles* and *Introduction to Mathematical Philosophy*. I discovered "On Denoting" while looking at old copies of *Mind* in the Sterling Library. Russell remains a primary philosophical influence.

We were free to take whatever courses or tutorials were available in and out of the department. I audited mathematics courses taught by some of the strong mathematics faculty and enrolled in a six-day-a-week, yearlong course in theoretical physics required of first-year graduate physics students: five lectures with a test on Saturday. The major philosophy-department requirement was the preliminary examination; a five- (or was it six?) day series of examinations in the "fields" of philosophy. It was a marathon. I've watched, with some rue, the requirement disappear.

With Fitch's approval, I began to work on a dissertation proposal. There was an entrenched belief that there were insurmountable difficulties of interpretation with extending modal propositional logic to include quantification. I did not see such insurmountable difficulties.

My plan was to develop rigorous axiomatic extensions of some of Lewis's systems to include quantification. Problems of interpretation could then be discussed relative to the framework. Meanwhile, as I worked on the prospectus, the Second World War was escalating, and science departments were increasingly shorthanded as faculty departed for war-related research. I was persuaded to take on grading for the graduate theoretical-physics course, for which I received $550. I then learned that the amount had to be deducted from my miniscule fellowship. (Yale largesse.) Grading that course was an ordeal. The language of physics was not my native tongue.

There was an influx of Reserve Officer Training candidates, and my husband, who was a physics graduate student, was appointed "instructor." Yale wheels began to grind. Since I was now a faculty wife, however accidental, a gorgeous bouquet was delivered. The provost's wife called and left an engraved card. I had cards engraved and returned the call. I still have the remaining cards.

By the fall of 1943, my dissertation prospectus, "A Strict Functional Calculus," was approved. In 1944, we moved to the Washington, D.C., area, where my husband was now engaged in military research at the Johns Hopkins Applied Physics Laboratory. I completed the dissertation in absentia, using the Library of Congress as needed. The library was in disarray, and when a request for a book or journal, like the *Journal of Symbolic Logic*, was delayed, the explanation would be that members of Congress had special borrowing privileges.

I mailed sections to Fitch for perusal. He finally said I had done enough and suggested that I immediately submit an initial part on first-order modal quantification theory for publication in the *Journal of Symbolic Logic*, which I did. It was accepted without delay by the then editor Alonzo Church, published in *JSL* 11[9] and reviewed the same year (1946).[10]

With the end of the war, I returned to New Haven. My dissertation was actually ready for submission in 1945, but it was submitted for the 1946 deadline. Church accepted two other papers for *JSL*: one on the deduction theorem in first-order modal quantification theory[11] and one on second-order modal quantification with identity, in which the necessity of identity was proved.[12] That resulted in a stir since, at the time, the existence of contingent identities was a received view.

Church, noting my Russellian dispositions, then asked me to review a paper of Arthur Smullyan, who defended an early Russellian solution to substitution puzzles in modal contexts.[13] I defended Smullyan in turn.[14] It was about the time of the review request (my recollection is fuzzy here) when Church informed me testily that he had learned I was married and must heretofore use my "legal" name on papers submitted to the *Journal of Symbolic Logic*. I acquiesced.

A word about publication: I am not driven to publish. Papers are submitted where I think I have a useful account of or solution to a clear question of logical or philosophical interest. The questions usually originate in some commonsense observations, couched in our common, ordinary language. It is therefore disappointing when blatant errors about what I have done occur and persist. I mean literal errors—not disagreements about interpretation. In the case of the paper on identity, for example, a major result and its import were missed by the reviewer. I expected the error would be noticed and corrected, but after eleven years of expectation, during which the error had been carried along by others in the literature, I wrote to the reviewer, who then informed Church: "A grave and puzzling error in my review XII 95(4) of Miss Barcan has just come to my attention. It is ancient history, but still I'd feel relieved if you could see your way to publishing a signed correction." A correction was published in *JSL* 23. Misreadings and neglect of some later work continued but not uniformly. Some misreadings and omissions were corrected, some escalated into controversies, and some results were ignored. My keen disappointment was that my romantic notions about the self-correcting feature of research within a scholarly community were not a given. There remain lengthy bibliographies and historical accounts of intensional and modal logic as well as interpretations of modalities where reference to my work is absent, but that is gradually being corrected.

Returning now to my recollections, we were back in New Haven, where my husband began a dissertation in low-temperature physics. In the absence of local teaching opportunities, I took a research position at the Yale Institute for Human Relations. The institute, funded by the Rockefeller Foundation, was dominated by Freudians, and an orthodox analysis was required for some PhD candidates in psychology and social anthropology. Yale was also a center for the study of behaviorism, under Clark Hull. I was recruited to participate in two areas of research which were being pursued. First, the attempt to verify some psychoanalytic hypotheses cross-culturally, such as relating childhood trauma to irrational adult explanations of illness in cultures without scientific medicine. Several of us participated. There was secondly, turned over to me, a project of synthesizing psychoanalytic and behavioral theory. Neither project was a success. Thinned out results were finally published in a book by J. Whiting and I. Child, *Child Training and Personality*, in which I am described as a "contributor and critic of concepts."[15] But I welcomed the opportunity to study psychology and social anthropology.

With PhDs granted, we were off to Chicago with post-doctoral fellowships, mine from the American Association of University Women. It was for me an opportunity to study with Carnap. Carnap was also concerned with modalities and quantification, but we were in strong disagreement. In his modal language, individual terms had dual reference; in the scope of a modal operator, the referent was an intension (an individual concept)—something that I was at pains to resist. I welcomed an opportunity to discuss our differences.

A day after arrival, I inquired at the University of Chicago about making suitable arrangements. The chair of the department gave me Carnap's home address. It seems he met students at home and rarely frequented the department. The atmosphere was strained. Carnap's autobiographical remarks, published in the Schilpp volume on Carnap, are revealing. He says of a departmental discussion, "I had the weird feeling that I was sitting among a group of medieval learned men . . . and would dream that one of my colleagues raised the famous question of how many angels could dance on the point of a needle."[16] Such a remark might suggest that Carnap lacked appreciation for the history of philosophy, which was clearly false. He did believe that analytic philosophy had made important advances worthy of consideration but which were not regarded as such by many of his colleagues. Some junior faculty warned me, in jest, that if the Chicago department invited me to give a talk I might be asked whether my views were to be found in Nicholas of Cusa.

I joined some young scholars who met regularly in Carnap's flat. They gathered around him. (He was prone due to a back ailment.) Some of the graduate students, for example, Dick Jeffrey, believed that completing a dissertation under Carnap would be thwarted by the department. Jeffrey transferred to Princeton. I was rapidly learning that

departments were not the peaceful communities of scholars I had fanta-
sized.

After two years, we moved north to Evanston, Illinois, where my
husband joined the Northwestern University physics department.
Northwestern at the time had a nepotism rule, which excluded regular
appointment of spouses. In any case, I did not seek a regular position.
My publications were well received. I had some courtesy privileges and
was invited to participate in the colloquia of the department and to
teach an occasional course as a "visiting professor." In 1952, I was
awarded a Guggenheim Fellowship. Between 1959 and 1962, I continued to think about modalities and intensional languages informally and
formally as well as interpretively. I also taught part-time at Roosevelt
College (named after FDR) in Chicago. It was originally a YMCA urban
school, but, when faced with racist demands, the administration and
most faculty agreed to secede from the Y. It then occupied one of the
architectural marvels designed by Louis Sullivan: the Auditorium Hotel
overlooking Lake Michigan.

There was, astonishingly, no state-supported four-year college in
Chicago. A comprehensive university was projected, but political wran-
gling delayed it for many years. It was a matter of competing for many
millions of dollars and acres of Chicago real estate, which impinged on
ethnic neighborhoods. A temporary junior college of the University of
Illinois system had been established on Navy Pier, which was supposed
to transition into the college, but the project languished.

My research job at Yale had stimulated an interest in psychoanalysis,
and I was accepted as a "control" at the Chicago Psychoanalytic Institute, meeting four times a week with an analyst-in-training. Interesting
as it was, my research at Yale and my orthodox analysis were consistent
with the later conclusions of Grünbaum et al: psychoanalysis as theory
or clinical practice would not bear scientific scrutiny.

I was in communication with philosophers who were based in the
area and those who visited. There was Leonard Linsky in the Chicago
department with whom I had many fruitful and continuing discussions.
He later included my paper "Extensionality" in the Oxford Readings,
Reference and Modality.[17] During that period, I met David Kaplan
when he visited Chicago. He has remained a very insightful critic and a
fast and loyal friend. Arthur Prior gave a seminar at the University of
Chicago in 1962, which I attended. I believe it was Prior who coined

the term "Barcan formula" for an axiom about the mingling of modal operators and quantifiers, about which debate continues.

In 1961, the Boston Colloquium in Philosophy of Science invited me to present the paper "Modalities and Intensional Languages." Quine's negative views had been expressed immediately on the heels of my publications, in his *JSL* reviews of 1946 and 1947 as well as an article, "The Problem of Interpreting Modal Logic," also in the 1947 volume of *JSL*, where he considers "the systems of Miss Barcan."[18] It was as if such efforts needed to be nipped in the bud. My address was published in *Synthese* in 1961 and presented in February 1962 with comments by Quine.[19] The entire proceedings was published in *Boston Studies in Philosophy of Science* along with some much edited further discussion by Quine, Føllesdal, Kripke, and McCarthy.[20] I was apprehensive about the colloquium. My name is Ruth, and I was in alien corn: the Harvard Faculty Club.

There is, on my account, no inflated metaphysics of possible worlds, except as a *façon de parler*. Possibility is about the way the actual world might be. Three axiomatic extensions of Lewis's systems with quantifiers are considered. The domain of interpretation consists of actual individuals. A theory of direct reference is proposed for proper names of individuals. They do not change reference in the scope of modal operators as in Carnap. Descriptions do not refer directly—they describe. They function like predicates or attributes. There are no possibilia (possible individuals). Possibility is about properties actual things might or do have. A modal language will accommodate talk of essential attributes, i.e., necessary but not logically necessary attributes, but may be consistent with the falsehood of all essentialist claims—a conclusion. I intuited, and Terry Parsons later proved in "Essentialism and Quantified Modal Logic."[21] But I saw nothing amiss in what is genuine "Aristotelian essentialism," which Quine characterized as "invidious." Aristotelian essentialism is about essential properties—not about individual essences. Candidates for essential attributes were, as I understood it, physically necessary properties: those covered by physical or, more broadly, empirical law. They are not metaphysical. I do tend to call "metaphysical" some high-level physical laws, such as the one Einstein proposes in the special theory of relativity: laws of physics are the same when determined relative to one inertial system as when determined relative to any other.

An aside: The question which baffled Russell was how an ordinary proper name could retain its reference over time, where there is no direct access to the object named. My thought was that Russell should not have abandoned what seemed to be his earlier acceptance of direct reference for proper names (e.g., "Scott"), although how that could be (i.e., direct reference over time) was not yet explained. Russell later identified "logically" proper names with a pointing, accompanying "this" and "that," and interpreted ordinary proper names as disguised descriptions: a backward move. The first satisfactory answer to Russell's question was, to the extent that I can determine, that of Geach several years later in "The Perils of Pauline," where he sets out the historical chain theory:

> For the use of word as a proper name there must in the first instance be someone acquainted with the object named. But language is an institution . . . and the use of a name for a given object . . . like other features of language, can be handed down from one generation to another. . . . Plato knew Socrates, and Aristotle knew Plato, and Theophrastus knew Aristotle and so on in apostolic succession to our own time; that is why we can legitimately use "Socrates" as a name the way we do.[22]

Prior to Geach, I had dug my heels in. It was commonly claimed that lexicographers said of proper names that they had no "lexical meaning," but they, too, to the extent I could determine, gave no answer to Russell's question. Nor did I. I was persuaded to the point of stubbornness that one would surely be forthcoming. It was, in the historical chain theory of Geach, later alternatively (but less perspicuously) described as a causal theory of names.[23] Quine, in his response to my talk, dismissed the direct-reference view as a "red herring."

In August 1962, following the February Boston Colloquium, through the good offices of von Wright and Hintikka, an international "Colloquium on Modal and Many Valued Logics" was mounted in Helsinki, sponsored by the International Union of History and Philosophy of Science. A proceedings was published in *Acta Philosophica Fennica* (1963), which included papers by Åqvist, Geach, Halldén, Hintikka, Kripke, Lemmon, Montague, Prior, Rasiowa, Rescher, and Smiley, all of which would be of interest to those concerned with modalities.[24] I presented a paper on sets and attributes (later revised for improved vocabulary). The colloquium was exciting and productive. A cottage industry on modalities was launched and continues.

Meanwhile, the University of Illinois in Chicago had settled on a location and an architecturally avant-garde campus rose on what was an embattled ethnic Greek neighborhood. A search was launched in 1963 for departmental chairs, and I was approached. It seems I was not a unanimous choice of the search committee. The protest was that there never had been a woman chair at the University of Illinois! But it happened, and I embarked on one of my careers as a proper "professional." In a short time, we had a strong and congenial faculty, including (in senior and mid-level positions) George Dickie, Arnold Levison, Terence Parsons, Brian Skyrms, William Tait, Irving Thalberg, and Paul Ziff. Also, more junior, Fred Feldman, Paul Teller, and Rudolf Grewe. Ian Hacking came one term a year. Two instructors with de facto tenure as well as a young, able, feminist "continental" philosopher, Sandra Bartky, from Navy Pier were invited to join. There were other able adjunct appointments, such as Marcia Eaton. Money was raised to improve library holdings. Those holdings were enhanced by our purchase of Cassirer's personal library. Our plans for a graduate program were closely scrutinized by external examiners and approved. Initially, graduate students from the University of Chicago were recruited as graduate assistants. We decided not to employ Straussian graduate students from the University of Chicago Committee on Social Thought, who taught an esoteric code for deciphering philosophy texts. But soon enough, we had our own graduate students. Our first two PhDs were Nancy Cartwright and Vivian Well. The Society for Women in Philosophy was organized under Sandra Bartky's initiative. It became, and remains, a strong department.

Another of my parallel "careers" was participation in the work of our professional associations. In 1961, Charles Stevenson, then at Michigan, requested my services as secretary of the Western (now Central) Division of the APA. I was prompted to take it on by an awareness of the extent to which practices of professional associations impinged on their constituencies. Employment practices needed reform. Other demands on professional associations, such as evaluations of programs, defending the rights of its members, and the like, needed to be scrutinized. I continued serving the APA for fifteen years, some of it in the Central Division, including the office of president, and concluded with two terms, totaling six years, as chairman of the National Board of Officers in 1982. The association was transformed on the national level into a constitutionally defined professional association. The old-boy system of recruitment was transformed and reforms initiated. Standing committees on a range of issues concerning philosophers and philosophy were established.

Between 1963 and 1986, I also held various offices in the Association of Symbolic Logic, serving as vice president 1980–83 and president 1983–86.

Between 1960 and 1980, other papers I wrote which were of significant interest were "Dispensing with Possibilia," "Iterated Deontic Modalities," "Essentialism in Modal Logic," "Quantification and Ontology," "Nominalism and the Substitutional Quantifier," and "Essential Attribution." A paper titled "Moral Dilemmas and Consistency" had a surprising impact and is included in many collections on ethics. It argues inter alia that on logical accounts of consistency, moral dilemmas need not be a mark of inconsistency of a moral code.[25]

In 1970, Northwestern abandoned its nepotism rule and invited me to join the department. It was decidedly a "continental" department with the very able Sam Todes and William Earle as colleagues. Hilary Putnam came from UCLA on his first appointment but left after a year. Shortly after I joined, I received calls from Yale. There had for many years been steady departures of faculty from Yale: in 1967, Wilfrid Sellars, along with Alan Anderson, Nuel Belnap, and Jerry Schneewind and followed by Rich Thomason, decamped for Pittsburgh, where they became the core of a continuing strong program.

Kingman Brewster, the then Yale president, urged me to come and help rebuild the department. In 1972, I finally agreed and arrived in 1973. Memories in New Haven were still vivid of the protest against the Vietnam War and the shutdown of the Yale campus due to the trial of black activists.

I was one of three tenured faculty women. Although upper-division women had been admitted as undergraduates, the admission of lower-division women and the equalization of numbers and facilities were still being debated. Faculty meetings were tense. Yale had been long self-described as educating "Leaders of Men." There was protracted discussion of the need for hair dryers and separate bathrooms and the attendant costs. Over time, women came to be admitted on a more equal basis. Women's Studies and various programs and facilities for women were established. Mory's was liberated.

The Yale philosophy department was unsettled. Stephan Körner remained until retirement. Robert Fogelin left after fourteen years. Sarah Broadie came and then left for Princeton. Bob Adams came, served as chair, and then left for Oxford. It was only partly the result of a continental divide. Despite many handsome competing offers, I stubbornly stayed.

The dominant presences in the humanities at Yale were de Man, Derrida, and deconstruction. Derrida was sponsored by de Man, the reigning guru of the comparative literature department. The *New York Times* ran a magazine story pro and con, "The Tyranny of the Yale Critics," which included a sample of deconstructionist interpretation. A popular critic wrote, in a letter to the editor, that he thought the sample was the answer to the previous week's Double-Crostic.[26] Derrida was a recurrent visitor in Comparative Literature, but Philosophy resisted a joint appointment. The expressed negative views of John Searle and me earned us a footnote in Derrida's book *Limited Inc*. He describes us as "members of an academic Interpol."[27] With the disclosure that de Man had written extensively for a Belgium newspaper sympathetic to Nazism and had invented a fanciful persona in the United States as a putative émigré from the Belgium underground, deconstruction left Yale.

Despite the unevenness in the philosophy department, it was my professional home. However, I moved about: the Stanford Center for Advanced Study in the Behavioral Sciences, '78–'79; fellow of Wolfson College, Oxford, Trinity terms '85–'86; Clare Hall, Cambridge, Trinity term 1988, where I was made a permanent member of the Common Room. I enjoyed a stimulating term at UCLA. There were two summers as a guest of the Rockefeller Foundation's residence for scholars on Lake Como. In 1973, I was elected to the Institut International de Philosophie, proceeding through various offices, including president 1989–92 and, presently, president honoraire. I attended its far-flung meetings. I was, for several years, a member of the Steering Committee of the International Federation of Philosophical Societies. In all of these excursions, I encountered philosophers with whom I could profitably exchange views. I also encountered many ideological differences and disagreements and the degree to which political differences impinged on the scholarly profession. I'll cite two examples, out of many. I was program chairman of the Seventh International Congress of Logic, Methodology, and Philosophy of Science, held in Salzburg, Austria, from July 11 to July 16, 1983. G. E. Minc, of the Soviet Union, was invited by the section on model theory and proof theory to submit a paper, which he did, on applications of proof theoretic transformation. Dr. Minc had previously requested emigration from the Soviet Union and had been consequently relieved of his research position. We were informed that since he was unemployed he was denied exit to attend the conference. The bylaws of the International Union require that all scholars have free mobility to and from conferences, but my efforts at gaining him a visa from the Soviet authorities were not successful. Professor Feferman agreed to read Minc's paper, but at a meeting of the program committee, Russian delegates said there was no rule which permitted someone's paper to be read. It was heatedly debated, but we pointed out there was ample precedent for this being done, and finally Feferman did deliver Minc's paper. After the meeting, several of us tried to help Minc in his efforts to emigrate. He finally succeeded and is presently a professor in the Stanford mathematics department. Nor is it the case that the United States was free from such decisions. Iris Murdoch told me that in 1946 she was denied a visa to this country, and subsequently refused invitations to visit the United States, excepting one occasion on which she was invited to lecture and was granted a restricted visa confined to the city in which she was to lecture. One case among many in the United States during the 1940s and subsequent years.

A high point was an invitation to lecture at the College de France in 1986—an interesting institution. The college was originally established by Francis I with the purpose of bringing France up to a higher standard of research, which had been thwarted at the Sorbonne. The lectures are advertised throughout Paris, and many of the audience come in off the street. There were stern ladies who knit like Madame Defarge. I apologized for having to lecture in English but was excused since, as I was told, "The last American who lectured at the College only *thought* he was speaking French."

I served on panels of the National Science Foundation, the National Endowment for the Humanities, the Rockefeller Foundation, the Fulbright Committee, and the Committee for Philosophy of the Educational Testing Service. We recommended that the Educational Testing Service abandon the philosophy test. There were frequent strange imbalances in that test: one year, for example, an inordinate number of questions concerned Paul Tillich, whereas major figures were neglected.

From 1979 onwards, I served as a visitor and evaluator of programs at many universities, including Princeton, MIT, Columbia, Caltech, Duke, University of Massachusetts–Amherst, and some University of California campuses. I also gave invited lectures and participated in conferences in the United States and abroad. The APA mounted a session on my work. Many further details of my "career" are here omitted, lest this memoir read like a laundry list. Among papers written after 1980, there are three on belief and believing, which are critical of the dominant language-centered view of belief and suggest some revisionary proposals. Of some interest is a study of Quine's animadversions on modalities and one on Russell's views of particularity.

It is true that the Yale department was fragile, but the students were a joy. I taught introductory philosophy in a special program for freshman, undergraduate survey courses in ethics, two or three levels of logic, and diverse advanced courses. I cherish the letters of thanks from students over the years. It is they who deserve thanks for the pleasure and stimulation they afforded. Some of the undergraduates I remember went on to careers in philosophy. Among those I recall are Tim Maudlin, Jessica Moss, Adina Roskies, Chris Smeenk, and Susan Wolf. Some of my graduate students are distinguished professors: Walter Sinnott-Armstrong, Nick Asher, Frank Farrell, Don Garrett, and Diana Raffman. Sinnott-Armstrong, in collaboration with Raffman and Asher, edited a Festschrift, *Modality, Morality and Belief*.[28]

Philosophers from whose views I have profited (although we are often in disagreement) are, in addition to those already mentioned, Nuel Belnap, Paul Benacerraf, Max Cresswell, Kit Fine, Robert Fogelin, Pat Greenspan, Henri Lauener, Isaac Levi, Charles Parsons, Terry Parsons, Ori Simchen, Ernest Sosa, Bob Stalnaker, Judy Thomson, and David Wiggins. But I am essentially a loner. One of the changes in academic style in recent years is the distribution of papers by an author for comment by large, sometimes astonishingly large, numbers of contemporaries, which is then noted in the acknowledgments. That was not my style. There was often no point, in any case, since I characteristically defended positions contrary to received views, if there were received views. I resist the pigeonholing philosophical taxonomy such as "materialist," "idealist," "realist," "dualist," "functionalist," "internalist," "physicalist," etc. I find myself in support of Pen Maddy's low key "naturalistic views" as given in *Second Philosophy: A Naturalistic Method*.[29] And I do use the term, as in the paper "The Anti-Naturalism of Some Language Centered Accounts of Belief."[30]

Mandatory retirement came in 1992. A collection of essays, *Modalities*, was published by Oxford.[31] The many critical reviews were favorable beyond expectation. I continued to teach an occasional course at Yale, and I visited the University of California at Irvine for some consecutive years, one term a year, with pleasure and profit. After 1998, I no longer traveled abroad with the exception of a trip to Bern in May 2008 for an International Symposium on Analytical Philosophy in my honor, sponsored by the Lauener Foundation. Henri Lauener was a colleague and member of the International Institute of Philosophy who edited a Festschrift published in *Dialectica* (1999).[32] There were challenging papers, to which I have still to respond. There was music, an address by Professor Essler, who is president of the foundation, and a head-turning "laudatio" by Tim Williamson.

Before closing, I want to express my gratification at the present benign state of the Yale department after many years during which I began to despair. It is Michael Della Roca, a fine philosopher and unparalleled administrator, who has chaired for over six years and steered the department to its present level of distinction—a Sisyphean task. My thanks finally to the APA for inviting me to give this lecture and my thanks to all of you for your patience.

✿ ✿ ✿

Ruth Barcan Marcus died in 2012. That year at a memorial event at Yale University, Judith Jarvis Thomson offered the following remarks.

Whenever I saw Ruth again after a lapse of some months, I was always struck at first by how small she actually was. I always remembered her as big—and big she always seemed. She had a big voice and a big gurgling laugh. She didn't have any small attitudes: when she was pleased by a thing, she loved it, and when she was displeased by a thing, she loathed it. She had more energy than any three of us, and she never left you in doubt where she stood.

We go back many years. I first met Ruth in 1965, I think, through James Thomson, who had met her at a conference. James had had an offer from the University of Chicago; Ruth had been invited to build a department of philosophy at Chicago Circle, and on James's and my visit to have a look at Chicago, she suggested that I join her there. We talked a lot about that idea, but for a variety of reasons, our move to Chicago didn't work out, and Ruth soon left Chicago Circle anyway.

But that was when our talk began, and it went on, with longer and shorter lapses for over forty years.

We talked about philosophy, of course. Not often about her work since I'm not at home in the areas she worked in, rather about mine or, more often, about papers that one or other of us had recently read or heard presented. She liked to keep track of what was going on in philosophy generally. She had strong views, of course, and some ideas that got floated simply enraged her. But she loved the practice of philosophy—she was fascinated by all of it.

We also talked about the administration of philosophy. At length about her difficulties in the philosophy department at Yale, of course, but also at length about the American Philosophical Association and about the question of what role it should play in the philosophy community. She greatly enjoyed serving on departmental visiting committees, and she was in much demand for them.

And, of course, we shared academic gossip. Ruth was the primary source: she knew everybody, she cherished the ridiculous, and she was a splendid mimic. Ruth's oldest and closest friend—in the philosophy world anyway—was Mary Mothersill. Mary had a lovely dry wit, and she and Ruth competed for the honor of giving the most devastating description of a bit of absurd behavior exhibited at some meeting or convention. They competed in other ways too. They played fast tennis at Mary's house in Bridgehampton, and then they played fast badminton by way of resting after tennis.

Mary came to call the three of us "Old Ladies Lib." It was plain that the situation of women in philosophy was improving, but it was improving far too slowly. Ruth herself played an important role in the lives of many women. She advised, she encouraged, she praised. She took active steps: she made phone calls and wrote letters—and letters and then more letters—in support of promotions, fellowships, and tenure. And, of course, she was a stellar role model.

It calls for mention that she liked many of the things traditionally thought of as feminine. She liked to cook dinner, and she liked there to be flowers on the table. She had a good eye for good clothes; she dressed well and liked to see others dressed well. It was very satisfying that she should combine those likes with intense commitment to philosophy.

While on the subject of things traditionally thought of as feminine, it is essential to draw attention to the fact that while she was on stage doing all of the things she is known for—writing philosophy and presenting it at meetings of various kinds, contributing to the administration of philosophy, helping women in philosophy—she was also backstage quietly raising four children. Academic women of our generation didn't have children; it took all the time and energy you had to make a place for yourself and to help other women do so too. The rare exceptions had one child. Nobody had four—surely four wasn't possible! Ruth did it, though. Her life was impossibly rich and thick.

It's a great pity that we can't telephone her, now that the speeches have all been made. She'd want to know who's here and what was said. And then, after we'd told her, the familiar big voice would say thanks, that's very nice, but look, so-and-so over-assessed such and such, and don't you agree that so-and-so-other under-assessed such and such and that so-and-so-still-other drew the wrong conclusion from the wrong data. That was her style. One can almost hear her voice in it. She's irreplaceable.

NOTES

John Dewey Lecture delivered before the 106th annual Eastern Division Meeting of the American Philosophical Association in New York, New York, on December 29, 2009. Used by permission of the John Dewey Foundation.

1. Rudolf Carnap, "On the Character of Philosophic Problems," *Philosophy of Science* 1, no. 1 (January 1934): 6.

2. Arthur O. Lovejoy, *The Great Chain of Being: A Study of the History of an Idea* (Cambridge, MA: Harvard University Press, 1936).

3. James Burnham and Philip Wheelwright, *Introduction to Philosophical Analysis* (New York: Henry Holt, 1932).

4. James Burnham, *The Managerial Revolution: What Is Happening in the World* (New York: John Day, 1941).

5. James Burnham, *The Machiavellians, Defenders of Freedom* (New York: John Day, 1943).

6. Albert Hofstadter and J. C. C. McKinsey, "On the Logic of Imperatives," *Philosophy of Science* 6, no. 4 (October 1939): 446–57.

7. David Hilbert and Paul Bernays, *Grundlagen der Mathematik* (Berlin: Springer, 1934).

8. Edgar S. Furniss, *The Graduate School of Yale: A Brief History* (New Haven, CT: Carl Purington Rollins Printing-Office, 1965), 73.

9. Ruth C. Barcan, "A Functional Calculus of First Order Based on Strict Implication," *Journal of Symbolic Logic* 11, no. 1 (March 1946): 1–16.

10. W. V. Quine, review of "A Functional Calculus of First Order Based on Strict Implication," by Ruth C. Barcan, *Journal of Symbolic Logic* 11, no. 3 (September 1946): 96–97.

11. Ruth C. Barcan, "The Deduction Theorem in a Functional Calculus of First Order Based on Strict Implication," *Journal of Symbolic Logic* 11, no. 4 (December 1946): 115–18.

12. Ruth C. Barcan, "The Identity of Individuals in a Strict Functional Calculus of Second Order," *Journal of Symbolic Logic* 12, no. 1 (March 1947): 12–15.

13. Arthur Francis Smullyan, "Modality and Description," *Journal of Symbolic Logic* 13, no. 1 (March 1948): 31–37.

14. Ruth C. Barcan, review of "Modality and Description," by Arthur Francis Smullyan, *Journal of Symbolic Logic* 13, no. 3 (September 1948): 149–50.

15. J. W. M. Whiting and I. Child, *Child Training and Personality: A Cross-Cultural Study* (New York: Yale University Press, 1953).

16. Paul Arthur Schilpp, *The Philosophy of Rudolf Carnap*, The Library of Living Philosophers 11 (La Salle, IL: Open Court, 1963).

17. Leonard Linsky, *Reference and Modality*, Oxford Readings in Philosophy (London: Oxford University Press, 1971).

18. Quine, review of "A Functional Calculus"; W. V. Quine, review of "The Identity of Individuals in a Strict Functional Calculus of Second Order," by Ruth C. Barcan, *Journal of Symbolic Logic* 12, no. 3 (September 1947): 95–96 (Corrected in *JSL* 1958); W. V. Quine, "The Problem of Interpreting Modal Logic," *Journal of Symbolic Logic* 12, no. 2 (June 1947): 43–48.

19. Ruth Barcan Marcus, "Modalities and Intensional Languages," *Synthese* 13, no. 4 (December 1961): 303–22; W. V. Quine, "Reply to Professor Marcus," *Synthese* 13, no. 4 (December 1961): 323–30.

20. Marx Wartofsky, ed., *Proceedings of the Boston Colloquium for the Philosophy of Science, 1961/1962*, Boston Studies in the Philosophy of Science 1 (Dordrecht, Netherlands: Reidel, 1963), 77–112.

21. Terence Parsons, "Essentialism and Quantified Modal Logic," *Philosophical Review* 78, no. 1 (January 1969): 35–52.

22. Peter Geach, "The Perils of Pauline," *Review of Metaphysics* 23 (December 1969): 288–89.

23. See lecture 11 of Saul Kripke, "Naming and Necessity," in *Semantics of Natural Language*, ed. D. Davidson and G. Harman (Dordrecht, Netherlands: Reidel, 1972).

24. *Acta Philosophica Fennica*, vol. 16, 1963.

25. Ruth Barcan Marcus, "Dispensing with Possibilia," *Proceedings and Addresses of the American Philosophical Association* 49 (1975): 39–51; Ruth Barcan Marcus, "Iterated Deontic Modalities," *Mind*, n.s., 75, no. 300 (October 1966): 580–82; Ruth Barcan Marcus, "Essentialism in Modal Logic," *Noûs* 1, no. 1 (March 1967): 41–96; Ruth Barcan Marcus, "Quantification and Ontology," *Noûs* 6, no. 3 (September 1972): 240–50; Ruth Barcan Marcus, "Nominalism and the Substitutional Quantifier," *Monist* 61 (July 1978): 351–62; Ruth Barcan Marcus, "Essential Attribution," *Journal of Philosophy* 68, no. 7 (April 1971): 187–202; Ruth Barcan Marcus, "Moral Dilemmas and Consistency," *Journal of Philosophy* 77 (March 1980): 121–36.

26. Cohn Campbell, "The Tyranny of the Yale Critics," *New York Times*, February 9, 1986; Andrew A. Rooney, "Letter to the Editor," *New York Times*, March 16, 1986.

27. Jacques Derrida, *Limited Inc.* (Evanston, IL: Northwestern University Press, 1988).

28. Walter Sinnott-Armstrong, Diana Raffman, and Nicholas Asher, eds., *Modality, Morality and Belief: Essays in Honor of Ruth Barcan Marcus* (Cambridge: Cambridge University Press, 1995).

29. Penelope Maddy, *Second Philosophy: A Naturalistic Method* (New York: Oxford University Press, 2007).

30. Ruth Barcan Marcus, "The Anti-Naturalism of Some Language Centered Accounts of Belief," *Dialectica* 49, no. 2–4 (1995): 113–30.

31. Ruth Barcan Marcus, *Modalities: Philosophical Essays* (New York: Oxford University Press, 1995).

32. Henri Lauener, ed., *Dialectica* 53 (1999): 3–4.

5

THE ROMANCE OF PHILOSOPHY

Richard J. Bernstein

It seems appropriate to start with a time before I studied philosophy—indeed, before I even had the foggiest idea about philosophy, when I was a high-school student in Brooklyn. I grew up in a supportive, extended, second-generation Jewish immigrant family. Neither of my parents went to college, and among my many aunts and uncles, none of them had a college education except for one who became a lawyer—one of the two favored professions (along with medicine) for young Jewish boys growing up in the 1940s. I went to Midwood High School, a public high school in Brooklyn where I experienced an intellectual awakening. I discovered the joys of literature, music, and art. Many of you know more about Midwood High School than you realize; it is also the high school of Woody Allen. When my wife Carol—also a Midwood graduate—and I first saw the early Woody Allen movies, we couldn't quite understand why everyone else was laughing. After all, these were the local jokes we heard in high school. I was too young to be drafted into the Second World War, but the war touched my family deeply because my highly gifted older brother was killed just before I reached my thirteenth birthday. But growing up in New York was an exciting experience; it was an optimistic time—a time when many of us had a deep conviction that somehow we could make a significant difference in shaping a better America and a better world.

When it came time to select a college, a friend suggested that I apply to the University of Chicago. During the late forties and fifties, the undergraduate college at the University of Chicago was a unique place.

The entire undergraduate curriculum was fixed and required; there were no electives and no majors. The college accepted students after the sophomore year in high school, although I enrolled when I graduated from high school. Advancement was not by taking credit hours but by passing an examination for each of the required courses. And the culminating course had the modest title: Observation, Integration, and Interpretation of the Sciences. Upon entering the college, one took a series of placement tests in order to determine which examinations had to be passed in order to graduate with a BA. Imagine a college where all the students are reading and talking about the same books. During my first quarter, I was reading Herodotus, Thucydides, Plato, Aristotle, Weber, Galileo, Kepler, Dostoevsky, and Freud. It was a heady experience, and I recall many a night when we stayed up all night passionately arguing about the fine points in Plato or Aristotle. But none of this quite captures what Chicago was really like at the time. The rumor had spread through America that Chicago was the only place to go if one aspired to be a serious intellectual. We had a disdain for the Ivy League. And Chicago attracted a remarkably talented student body and faculty. Susan Sontag took the same section of social science with me with a young Chicago instructor, Philip Rieff. It was in Chicago that I met and became good friends with Dick Rorty. This was the Chicago of Philip Roth and Mike Nichols, as well as Allan Bloom and George Steiner. A. J. Liebling wrote a profile of Chicago, the Second City, for the *New Yorker* and referred to the University of Chicago as the greatest center for juvenile neurotics since the Children's Crusade. It was in Chicago that I discovered and fell in love with philosophy. And it was Plato's *Phaedrus* that turned me on. It is still my favorite piece of philosophy, and I have never lost my love for the Platonic dialogues.

I graduated from Chicago at the age of nineteen, but the only institutions at that time that would recognize a Chicago BA as a preparation for graduate study were Oxford and Cambridge. For personal reasons, because my family was still in mourning for the death of my brother, I decided to return to New York to study at Columbia for a couple of years before pursuing graduate studies. I took courses ranging from ancient Greek to book binding. (My mother thought I should study something "practical.") But I was already hooked on philosophy. The word from my Chicago friends was that one of the few places where one could seriously study philosophy in the spirit of Chicago was Yale. Dick

Rorty was the first of my friends to go to Yale from Chicago, and a number of us followed. When I went to Yale in 1953 to study philosophy, I never thought of myself as entering "the profession." I thought of myself as pursing an adventure in ideas. I felt the romance of the life of the mind, and I was still very naive. My first year of graduate school was, as I recall it, both thrilling and terrifying. Like many first-year graduate students, I wondered if I had made the right decision to pursue graduate studies in philosophy and whether I was really good enough. This came home to me in a particularly vivid way when I enrolled in a seminar on Hegel's *Phenomenology of Spirit*. I decided to take the course on Hegel because I had never read a word of Hegel and thought I should know something about him. But initially, the experience was traumatic. I did not understand a single word—and I could not understand how anybody else thought they could understand Hegel. I was intimidated because there were many advanced bright students in the class who seemed to talk very intelligently about Hegel— and I didn't know what was going on. I felt that this was a real test of my philosophic ability—and that I was failing it. I was terrified in anticipation of giving a class presentation. Surely everyone would realize that I was an idiot and did not belong in a graduate philosophy program. My assignment was the section in the *Phenomenology* where Hegel discusses the *Antigone*. I spent hours poring over the text, and somehow I had a breakthrough—like an epiphany. I experienced the power.

Next, I want to tell how I came to write my dissertation on John Dewey. It illustrates what I take to be one of the most important aspects of any graduate training—the significance of informal discussion groups that can turn out to be more important than the formal courses that one takes. I barely knew anything about Dewey before I went to Yale. And what I thought I knew about Dewey, I didn't like. Dewey allegedly epitomized everything that we had been taught to disdain at Chicago. A young Yale assistant professor, John E. Smith, organized a small informal reading group to discuss *Experience and Nature*, and I decided to join. *Experience and Nature* did not fit the stereotype of Dewey and pragmatism that were so popular at the time—and Dewey struck me as a much more interesting and important thinker. I felt a deep affinity with Dewey's vision of experience and nature and with his role as a public intellectual concerned with the character and destiny of radical democracy. The 1950s were probably the absolute low point of

any philosophic interest in Dewey and pragmatism, but I was sufficiently headstrong—or perverse—to write my dissertation on John Dewey's
metaphysics of experience. Much later, I discovered what Oliver Wendell Holmes Jr. said upon reading *Experience and Nature*. In a letter to
Frederick Pollock, he wrote, "Although Dewey's book is incredibly ill
written it seemed to me . . . to have a feeling of intimacy with the
universe that I found unequaled. So methought God would have spok-
en had He been inarticulate but keenly desirous to tell you how it was."
Because Paul Weiss, one of the editors of the *Collected Papers* of
Peirce, was a lively and forceful presence at Yale, I also started studying
Peirce. And some of my earliest publications were on Dewey and
Peirce.

The late forties and fifties were the time when a quiet but dramatic
revolution was taking place in graduate philosophy departments. Most
"respectable" departments were in the process of becoming analytic—
influenced by either the legacy of logical empiricism or the "ordinary
language" philosophy that was then practiced in Oxford. And it was
from this period that the infamous Anglo-American–Continental split
became entrenched. I went to Yale because it resisted this analytic
takeover, and frankly I never—not then or even today—thought in
terms of this split. I found Wittgenstein as exciting and fascinating as I
did Hegel, Nietzsche, and Kierkegaard—and I couldn't quite understand why the rest of the philosophic world did not think this way. Some
commentators have characterized my philosophic work as building
"bridges" between Anglo-American and Continental philosophy, but I
never thought of philosophic work in this way. No one and no style of
philosophizing has a monopoly on philosophic insight. There were no
"bridges" to be built. There is only good and bad philosophy—and there
is plenty of both on either side of the Atlantic. At Yale, I also studied
with Arthur Pap before his untimely death and with Peter Hempel
before he moved to Princeton. Hempel—contrary to the stereotypes of
logical empiricists—was one of the most humane and cultured teachers
that I ever had. Despite my early exposure to logical empiricism, I was
infected by an anti-analytic bias that was unfortunately encouraged at
Yale.

All this changed when Wilfrid Sellars joined the Yale faculty. I was a
young assistant professor when Sellars came to Yale, and I sat in on
many of his graduate courses during this highly creative period in his

own development. Sellars taught me how analytic finesse could deepen and clarify the philosophic problems that were at the heart of the great philosophic tradition. And to understand Sellars, one really had to master analytic philosophy of language, mind, action, and science—as well as a good deal of the history of philosophy. In 1966, I wrote one of the first comprehensive articles on Sellars's vision of man-in-the-world. Dick Rorty, as you know from *Philosophy and the Mirror of Nature*, shared my enthusiasm for Sellars. I have always made a sharp distinction between analytic ideology, which I find offensive and provincial, and the genuine fruits of analytic philosophizing. By analytic ideology, I am referring to the smug belief that the analytic style is the only game in town and the rest of philosophy is to be dismissed as simply not really worthwhile—not "really" philosophy. I recall how, in the fifties, the question was asked—frequently with a pseudo-Oxford accent—"Do you do philosophy or are you interested in the history of philosophy?" Anything other than some new turn on the latest discussions in *Mind*, *Analysis*, or the *Philosophical Review* simply didn't count as philosophy. This stifling ideology, which unfortunately still lurks in the hearts of some members of our "profession," is not only stupid and pernicious, but has much more to do with the boring game of academic politics than with serious philosophical thinking.

There is another aspect of my Yale experience that is important for understanding my development. I went to Yale during the height of the McCarthy period. Coming from the streets of Brooklyn and Chicago, I had very little idea of what the Ivy League was really like. And I was shocked. Yale, except for the graduate school, was an all-male institution, where undergraduates wore ties and jackets in the dining room. A large percentage of Yale undergraduates came from private schools and were sons of Yale alumni. Yale did admit a few women graduate students, but there were sections in the Yale Library that women were not permitted to enter—and, of course, no women were admitted to the famous eating place, Mory's. Yale was only just beginning to hire Jewish professors. Paul Weiss, in the philosophy department, was the first Jewish full professor appointed in the humanities. The great hero of Yale undergraduates at the time was the young William Buckley, who had recently published his scathing critique of Yale, *God and Man at Yale*. Frankly, I couldn't quite believe this was a real place and not a stage set for a Scott Fitzgerald novel. I already considered myself a left thinker strongly attracted to Dewey's radical vision of democracy, and I was attracted to the early humanistic readings of Karl Marx. (I taught one of the first courses on Marx offered in the Ivy League.) But gradually, things began to change—even at Yale. I served as the faculty advisor to the John Dewey Society, which later transformed into the SDS. And with the appointment of the new Yale chaplain, William Sloane Coffin, a small but vital group of faculty and students at Yale actively participated in the early civil rights movement and the anti–Vietnam War protests. In 1964, I joined a group of the Yale contingent that participated in the Mississippi Summer Project. I was asked to write about my experience for the *Nation*, and I would like to read something I wrote when I returned from Mississippi. Writing about voter registration of blacks (we used the word *Negroes* at the time), I described my experience witnessing the meeting where local blacks appointed delegates for the Freedom Democratic Party. This is what I wrote in 1964:

> The meeting was called to order at 4 o'clock on a sweltering Saturday afternoon. For the COFO workers this meeting was a test of what they had achieved. It was the point, they strongly felt, at which the local Negroes had to take over. Would they show up for the meeting? Would they make a mess of it? That meeting turned out to be one of the most impressive political gatherings that I have ever attended. Following parliamentary procedures, the session opened with a benediction, a keynote address, the democratic nomination and election of a permanent chairman and secretary, and proceeded to pass resolutions and appoint delegates to attend the district meeting. As the woman who was chairman said, we were all a little nervous because this sort of thing had never happened in Mississippi. It was the first political meeting open to everybody who wanted to come. Whenever in the future I think of what democracy can mean in the concrete, the image of that meeting in Eaton precinct will come to mind.

And today, more than fifty years after that meeting, it is still the image that comes to mind when I think of what democracy at its best really means.

In March 1965, I was denied tenure at Yale, and suddenly, I found myself involved in a famous tenure dispute. Two thousand students marched for me and for several days kept all-night vigils around the president's office—demanding reconsideration of my case. Dozens of

letters by philosophers and supporters from all over the country poured
into Yale. The story was picked up by the national media. I had the good
sense to keep my mouth shut and to stay away from the demonstrations,
but reports of what was happening at Yale were broadcast on all the
networks and written about in *Time*, *Newsweek*, and the *New York
Times*. I think the story got so much national publicity because this was
the first major student demonstration in the Ivy League; it was a time
when students were protesting that universities were stressing research
at the expense of fulfilling their mission as teaching institutions. I enjoyed some popularity as a teacher, although I also had begun publishing and had written a couple of books. The students carried placards
protesting my dismissal. And my favorite was the one that read, "Homer
Was A Two Book Man." Anyway, the media made me into some sort of
hero—and as a result, I was approached by thirty-six colleges and universities inquiring if I wanted to join their faculties. In order to tell the
truth and the whole truth, I should mention that just a few years ago,
David Crocker, who had been one of my teaching assistants in 1964,
told me that one of the students in the large introductory course I
taught was a very weak freshman by the name of George W. Bush.
When I discovered this, I told my own president at the New School,
Bob Kerrey, that Socrates was also famous for his failures.

When I left Yale, I was also the editor of the *Review of Metaphysics*.
Paul Weiss had founded the *Review of Metaphysics* in the 1940s. The
Review was run in a very unusual manner. Paul read all the submitted
manuscripts and made all the decisions about what to publish. Everyone who submitted a manuscript received a personal letter—regardless
of whether his or her manuscript was accepted or rejected. At a time
when many "prestigious" philosophic journals would publish only analytic articles, the *Review* was genuinely pluralistic. Quine, Sellars, and
Rorty, Leo Strauss, Hans Jonas, and even Heidegger were contributors
to the *Review*. Paul asked me to be managing editor and then assistant
editor when I was still in my twenties. I was never attracted by Paul
Weiss's grand style of metaphysical speculation, but few teachers had a
greater influence on me. Paul was the quickest and sharpest critic I ever
encountered. He could quickly detect the weakest point of any argument—and go for the jugular. When a manuscript was submitted to the
Review, I read it and wrote a comment. Then Paul read the manuscript
and my comment and ruthlessly critiqued what I wrote. It was a brutal

but wonderful education. One day, I walked into the office—fully ex-
pecting to be told what I had done wrong—and found a note from Paul.
"Dear Dick, I have taught you everything I can. The *Review* is now
yours." That's how I became editor. Paul's parting words were, edit the
journal as long as it is fun and you are learning something. And that is
what I did. After several years of editing the journal, I felt that I was no
longer learning anything new. All that was left was the prestige and
power of being an editor—so I gave it up.

When I had to seek a new job in the spring of 1965, I set one firm
condition. And that concerned my wife, Carol, who had gone to Swarthmore and received her PhD in English at Yale. She had been brought
up to believe that any career—including an academic career—would be
open to her. And although she did not experience any discrimination at
Swarthmore or as a graduate student at Yale, there were simply no
attractive opportunities to pursue an academic career in New Haven.
There seemed to be an unspoken attitude that—even with a Yale
PhD—a woman should find happiness in being married to someone on
the Yale faculty. So when I left Yale, I considered only those places
where Carol would also have an opportunity to independently pursue
her own career. I chose Haverford College because of the opportunities
for Carol in the Philadelphia area—and Carol soon started teaching at
the University of Pennsylvania and then accepted a position at Bryn
Mawr College—the sister college of Haverford. Some of my friends
were a bit perplexed that I decided to accept a position at an undergraduate college when I had the opportunity to go to a research university—especially because I had been teaching graduate and undergraduate students at Yale. But I was attracted to Haverford for many reasons—one of the best liberal-arts colleges in the country, Haverford
was founded by Quakers, and the Quaker legacy was still strong at
Haverford. There was a tradition of social concern. Haverford—unlike
most colleges and universities during the McCarthy period—refused on
principle to cooperate with the witch hunts. The Friends also took a
strong stand against the war in Vietnam. But what was most attractive
was the possibility of helping to build a vital philosophy department that
would stand at the center of the curriculum—one that would exemplify
the pluralistic conception of philosophy that I took to be fundamental
for education.

I don't know if any other liberal-arts college ever achieved what we achieved at Haverford. More students enrolled in philosophy courses than in any other discipline. Students would line up all night in order to get into our introductory courses. The heart of our curriculum was the encounter with the great philosophers. Our most popular seminars were seminars on Plato, Aristotle, Kant, Hegel, Heidegger, and Wittgenstein. When *Change* magazine came to Haverford to write up our program as one of the best undergraduate philosophy programs in the country, the article was entitled "Classical to the Core." I always considered myself a teacher-scholar and find as much satisfaction in teaching as I do in writing. During my time at Haverford, from 1966 until 1989, I published *Praxis and Action, The Restructuring of Social and Political Theory, Beyond Objectivism and Relativism,* and *Philosophical Profiles.* Let me quote something that I wrote in *Beyond Objectivism and Relativism*:

> There is a prevailing bias in the United States that liberal arts colleges are primarily teaching institutions and the university or multiversity is the place for serious scholarly research. But this bias (which, of course, contains some truth) can blind one to the unique advantages of liberal arts colleges for humanistic inquiry and scholarship. Humanistic studies, as their long tradition reveals, require an ambience where talk and dialogue are cultivated, where one feels free to pursue issues and problems that transgress conventional academic boundaries, and where one directly experiences the challenges and encounters that come from colleagues and students with diverse intellectual concerns. One of the primary reasons why I joined the faculty of Haverford College in the mid-1960s was that at a time when so many institutions of higher learning were experiencing the deleterious effects of excessive bureaucratization and professionalization, Haverford was still an educational community that honored the ideal of the teacher-scholar in word and deed.

Nineteen seventy-two was an especially important year in my development because that was the year that I met both Jürgen Habermas and Hannah Arendt. I had started reading Habermas in the 1960s, and when I read his book *Knowledge and Human Interests*, I experienced a shock of recognition. For many years, I had an interest in the Frankfurt School, and the distinctive Hegelian-Marxist orientation that influenced the early Frankfurt thinkers. Habermas was interested in the same range of thinkers that had fascinated me—Kant, Hegel, Marx, Peirce, Mead, Dewey, and Sellars. It is as if I, who started working in the pragmatic tradition and became increasingly interested in the Hegelian-Marxist legacy, were meeting Habermas, who, starting with the Hegelian-Marxist legacy, was moving closer to the spirit of pragmatism. His version of critical theory was very close to my understanding of critical pragmatism. I invited him to lecture at Haverford. When we met, we both felt a strong bond of intellectual friendship—one that has grown over the years. In 1976, Habermas spent a semester teaching at Haverford. And in 1988, I was a visiting professor at the University of Frankfurt. And just as earlier I had written one of the first comprehensive reviews of Sellars, so also Habermas figured prominently in my 1976 book, *The Restructuring of Social and Political Theory*.

When Habermas spent the semester at Haverford, he asked if I would join him in directing a seminar to be held in Dubrovnik in the spring. Tito, the Yugoslavian leader, had recently cracked down on the *Praxis* group in Yugoslavia—a group of humanistic Marxists who were sharply critical of Stalinist tendencies in communism. Eight professors belonging to the group had been dismissed from Belgrade University. They were forbidden to teach in Yugoslavia. Tito also closed the famous meetings at Korcula that had become a meeting place for left intellectuals from all over the world. And the journal *Praxis* was also forced to cease publication. Habermas and I considered it a gesture of solidarity to support our *Praxis* colleagues by conducting a short course at the Inter-University Centre. Ironically, this was the only site in Yugoslavia where the Belgrade *Praxis* group could give lectures. What started as a rather informal gesture of solidarity grew into an international institution. Over the years, a remarkable group of intellectuals participated in the Dubrovnik course, including Charles Taylor, Anthony Giddens, Steven Lukes, Dick Rorty, Cornelius Castoriadis, Alain Touraine, Albrecht Wellmer, Claus Offe, Ágnes Heller—the list goes on and on. And we attracted a most remarkable group of young graduate students, including Seyla Benhabib, Judith Butler, and Nancy Fraser. Let me read another passage from the preface to *Beyond Objectivism and Relativism*:

In the spring of 1978, I was traveling on the long flight from New York to Dubrovnik with a group of colleagues. Nancy Fraser, a close friend and former student of mine, who at the time was beginning to become interested in poststructuralist French thought, was pressing me about my philosophic work and where I really stood on basic issues. As our conversation became more intense and more heated (I felt I was being deconstructed), it turned to the question of objectivism and relativism. Challenged by Fraser's tenacious ability to get to the heart of issues, I blurted out that the dichotomy was pernicious; one needed to get beyond objectivism and relativism. Suddenly I realized that this was the focal point for which I had been searching. I spent the rest of the night outlining this book. One of the highlights of the 1978 Dubrovnik course was the participation of Richard Rorty. He read parts of what was later published as *Philosophy and the Mirror of Nature*, including the sections where he is critical of Jürgen Habermas and Charles Taylor (both of whom were present at this session). I had already read earlier drafts of Rorty's book and was at once sympathetic with his critique of foundationalism and extremely dubious about the conclusions he drew from this critique. We spent several stimulating sessions trying to sort out the differences that make a difference in our respective appropriations of the pragmatic tradition.

I mentioned that 1972 was also the year that I met Hannah Arendt. My colleague Sara Shumer in the political science department invited Arendt to give a lecture at Haverford. At the time, I was not much interested in Arendt, had scarcely read her work, and what I had read I didn't like because I thought her interpretation of Hegel and Marx was outrageous. (I still do.) I was prepared to thoroughly dislike her. But when she came to Haverford, she specifically asked to see me—although I hadn't the slightest idea why. Fred Wieck, the editor of my book *Praxis and Action*, had sent a copy to Hannah—and she wanted to tell me how much she liked the book. When we met at the Haverford Hotel, we spent six hours talking together. And that was the beginning of a friendship that lasted until her death in 1975. I sometimes think that the real reason why one publishes books is to dedicate them to family and friends—and I dedicated *Beyond Objectivism and Relativism* to four friends: Hannah Arendt, Hans-Georg Gadamer, Jürgen Habermas, and Richard Rorty. This is what I wrote about Hannah:

My first personal encounter with Hannah Arendt in 1972 was stormy. We had a sharp debate about our different interpretations of

Hegel and Marx. But that encounter was not only agonistic; it was also in Plato's sense, erotic. We met several times during the few remaining years of her life, and each time we passionately argued with each other. She is still very much a living presence for me, and I continue to argue with her.

I wrote that in 1983, but in 2006, I am still arguing with her. I want to mention one other aspect of our encounter that tells a great deal about Hannah. *Praxis and Action* was written long after *The Human Condition* and *On Revolution*. But as I indicated, I wasn't much interested in Arendt when I wrote the book, and there is only one insignificant footnote about Arendt in my book. But when we met, my failure to discuss Arendt's conception of action was of no interest to her. She wasn't at all concerned that I neglected to discuss her work. She praised my book because she felt that I was trying to do something fresh and original. In 1972, Arendt wanted me to join her at the New School, but I had little interest in doing so. My wife had a good teaching position, and we had four young children in good schools. New York was not only expensive but wasn't quite safe at the time. But, of course, I was quite flattered that she wanted me to join the faculty even though others at the New School were more skeptical of me.

I mentioned that the fourth friend to whom I dedicated *Beyond Objectivism and Relativism* was Hans-Georg Gadamer. I initially met Gadamer on his first visit to America in 1968. And I published what I believe was the first substantial critical study of *Truth and Method* in the *Review of Metaphysics*. During the time when Habermas and I taught our seminar in Dubrovnik, there was also another seminar dealing with phenomenology. Gadamer was a frequent visitor, and we had many discussions over a good bottle of wine in Dubrovnik. When Gadamer started his regular visits to the United States, he frequently visited Haverford. And increasingly, I felt myself influenced by—although also critical of—his hermeneutical orientation. My philosophic education, grounded in the pragmatic tradition, has always been one of reaching out to new encounters and new experiences, seeking to engage in genuine dialogue, and enlarging my own perspective.

In this respect, I want to mention one further philosophic friend, Jacques Derrida. Like many others, when I first started reading Derrida in the 1970s, I could not figure out what he was saying. I was irritated and annoyed at what struck me as pointless verbal word play. But my wife, Carol, was a great admirer of Derrida, and since I have great respect for my wife's intelligence, I felt there must be something there that I wasn't getting—and I kept at it. The breakthrough came when I read his magnificent essay on Lévinas, "Violence and Metaphysics." Somehow this essay did not fit with the popular image of Derrida as a verbal nihilist who had nothing much to say. I began to see that Derrida, from his earliest work, was preoccupied, indeed obsessed, with questions concerning ethics and responsibility. And I wrote an essay, "Serious Play: The Ethical-Political Horizon of Jacques Derrida." In 1987, Derrida was lecturing in the School of Criticism and Theory at Dartmouth. Geoffrey Hartman, a close friend from my Yale graduate days, was the director and invited me to meet Derrida. Derrida was pleased to meet a philosopher who appreciated the ethical-political dimension of his writings. I had recently been elected president-elect of the Eastern Division of the APA. And I asked Derrida if he would accept an invitation to the APA meeting when I was to give my presidential address. Now, as many of you know, analytic philosophers were not simply critical of Derrida, but they mocked and ridiculed him. When he visited the comparative literature department at Yale, philosophy students were discouraged from taking courses with him. I always thought this was scandalous—and violated my own deepest convictions about what serious critical philosophical engagement should be. Some of you may remember that session in December 1988 where more than a thousand persons attended his lecture. It was perhaps appropriate that Derrida gave a talk on the politics of friendship—the germ of his book with the same title. And the title of my presidential address was "Pragmatism, Pluralism, and the Healing of Wounds," where I wrote:

> The time has come to realize that there has been an ideological cultural lag in our profession—to realize that the ideological battles characteristic of the first wave of the reception of analytic philosophy in America no longer make much sense. The time has come to heal the wounds of these ideological battles. The time has come to realize how unilluminating and unfruitful it is to think in terms of Anglo-American/Continental split. The philosophic interminglings that are now taking place defy any simplistic dichotomy.

What I called for in that address is engaged fallibilistic pluralism where however much we are committed to our own styles of thinking, we are willing to listen to others without denying or suppressing the otherness of the other. It means being vigilant against the dual temptations of simply dismissing what others are saying by falling back on one of those standard defensive ploys where we condemn it as obscure, woolly, or trivial, or thinking we can always easily translate what is alien into our own entrenched vocabularies.

We frequently forget that the discussion of friendship formed a major part of the ethics and politics that has its roots in Aristotle. And the friendships that I have enjoyed with Dick Rorty, Hannah Arendt, Jürgen Habermas, Hans-Georg Gadamer, Jacques Derrida (and many others, including Agnes Heller and Yirmiyahu Yovel) have not only been a great source of joy that has enriched my life, they have also been the occasion for expanding my own philosophic horizons—of listening and learning from them and their texts. The best friendships are those where there is also friendly criticism—and I have been critical of all of these thinkers. But there is something else that attracted me to them— for all their diversity. Like my friend Dick Rorty, I think that the classical American pragmatists were really ahead of their time. Habermas, Arendt, Gadamer, and Derrida are *not* pragmatists and—with the exception of Habermas—they are barely familiar with the classical American pragmatists. Yet, I kept discovering themes in their work that bear a strong family resemblance to themes and to concerns central to the pragmatic thinkers. And in a number of my writings, I have sought to bring forth the themes in their work that are congenial to and enlarge a pragmatic orientation.

In 1989, I was invited to join the Graduate Faculty of the New School for Social Research after spending almost twenty-five happy and productive years at Haverford. Being New Yorkers, Carol and I always hoped to return to New York, and now that our youngest child went off to college, it became feasible. The New School was founded in 1919 as a consequence of protest at Columbia University. Nicholas Butler Murray, the president of Columbia, fired a young professor because he opposed the U.S. participation in the First World War. A group of Columbia University professors—including John Dewey—protested this gross violation of academic freedom and decided all to start a new institution that would break away from the taboos and types of discrimination that was so characteristic of "respectable" academic institutions of the time. The New School became a magnet for progressive social thinkers and avant-garde intellectuals. In 1933, Alvin Johnson, the president of the New School, decided to initiate the University in Exile—a refuge for those European professors and intellectuals who were forced to flee from Nazi Germany. This is the origin of the Graduate Faculty. The New School is a maverick institution. But it is perfectly suited to my philosophic interests and temperament. It prides itself in fostering an independent critical spirit. John Dewey was a founder of the New School. Horace Kallen, who coined the expression "cultural pluralism" and who was a student of William James, became one of the first philosophers to teach at the New School. The New School welcomed the émigré intellectuals from Europe (many of whom have had a profound influence on American culture). But the Graduate Faculty fell on hard times during the late 1970s, and several departments—including philosophy—had to suspend their PhD programs.

In the 1980s, when Jonathan Fanton became president, he made the decision to rebuild the Graduate Faculty. I was invited to help rebuild the philosophy department, and I served as chair from 1989 until 2002. Rebuilding philosophy at the New School presented a new challenge— to help shape a graduate philosophy department that would exemplify the open, engaged pluralism that has always marked my teaching and scholarship. Over the years, we have attracted a superb faculty and a lively, committed student body. Because most of our students have to work to help support themselves and undergo many sacrifices to come to the New School, their motivation is very high. At the New School, I was stimulated to expand my philosophical interests and scholarly work. I have written books on Arendt, Freud, and radical evil.

I want to conclude with a few general reflections. One of my favorite essays on education is Whitehead's essay "The Rhythm of Education," where he describes the rhythm of education as consisting of three interdependent stages: romance, precision, and generalization. "The stage of romance is the stage of first apprehension. The subject-matter has the vividness of novelty; it holds within itself unexplored connections with possibilities half-disclosed by glimpses and half-concealed by the wealth of material." What Whitehead means by romance is very close to Plato's Eros. This is what I experienced so vividly in those early days at Chicago—when so much of the excitement of life of the mind opened up for me. Romance needs to be followed by a second stage that Whitehead calls "precision." "In this stage, width of relationship is subordinated to exactness of formulation." Romance without precision is in danger of becoming sentimental; precision without romance too frequently becomes sheer pedantry. "It is evident," Whitehead declares, "that a stage of precision is barren without a previous stage of romance; unless there are facts which have already been vaguely apprehended in their broad generality, the previous analysis is an analysis of nothing. It is simply a series of meaningless statements about bare facts, produced artificially and without further relevance." The final stage, generalization, "is a return to romanticism with the added advantage of classified ideas and relevant technique. It is the fruition which has been the goal of the precise training." Whitehead describes a rhythm that ought to be reiterated throughout one's education and life. I sometimes think today that with the growth of the professionalism in our graduate schools we are in danger of losing the stage of romance—that Eros that is so essential for education. Or what is worse, although many of our students decide to pursue the study of philosophy because they have experienced its erotic attraction, we beat this out of them—placing all the emphasis on precision and sharpness of argumentation. Given all the pressures and worries that students confront about the "job market" and young assistant professors about getting "tenure"—there is little opportunity to indulge in romance. Yet I think Whitehead is right. Without romance, precision becomes pedantry and generalization impossible.

What Whitehead describes is equally applicable to one's own development. My own intellectual life follows the same pattern—and continues to do so. Over and over again, I have been fortunate to experience the romance of discovery—where some new problem or thinker opens up unexplored vistas and where there is "the sudden perception of half-disclosed and half-hidden possibilities." I try to stimulate this pattern of romance, precision, and generalization in my students. This is why—even after more than fifty years of teaching—it is still a thrill to enter the classroom.

Another good friend—and a friend of pragmatism—Hilary Putnam, was recently asked: what makes a good philosopher? He responded characteristically that one should recognize that there are many different types of good philosopher. But then he went on to add:

If one has to generalize, I would agree with Myles Burnyeat who once said that philosophy needs vision and arguments. Burnyeat's point was that there is something disappointing about a philosophy that contains arguments, however good, which are not inspired by some genuine vision, and something disappointing about a philosophic work that contains a vision, however inspiring, which is unsupported by arguments.

Putnam might have cited William James who made a similar point in *A Pluralistic Universe*. James employs a variety of ingenious arguments, but he declares that "a man's vision is the great fact about him. . . . Where there is no vision the people perish." And James warned that too many professional philosophers lack vision, but when a philosopher has vision, "one can read him over and over again, and each time bring away a fresh sense of reality."

My talk today has been retrospective, but as any good pragmatist knows, we look back on the past to understand the present and plan for the future. Little did I know when at the age of nineteen I decided to pursue a career in philosophy that more than fifty years later I would still feel the same thrill of excitement as I look forward to the opening of new possibilities, new students to teach, new problems to confront, and new vistas to explore.

NOTE

John Dewey Lecture delivered before the 103rd annual Eastern Division Meeting of the American Philosophical Association in Washington, D.C., on December 29, 2006. Used by permission of the John Dewey Foundation.

6

REFLECTIONS OF MY CAREER IN PHILOSOPHY

Harry Frankfurt

I

I graduated from college in 1949, I received my PhD in 1954, and then, after nearly two years in the Army of the United States, as a draftee during the Korean War, I started my first full-time academic job—at Ohio State University—in 1956. In those days, a massive post–Second World War boom in the academic world was continuing to move quite briskly along. Enormous numbers of military veterans—some still from the Second World War and others from the Korean War, all financially empowered by the generous educational benefits of the GI Bill—were flooding the country's higher education campuses. The demand for postsecondary education or training was continuing to increase, and the institutions of higher learning that then existed were simply insufficient to provide an adequate supply of the courses, the curricula, and the degrees and certifications that were urgently wanted.

So the supply of these items was systematically and liberally increased. New institutions and new campuses were created. Old colleges, which had previously been devoted to specialized purposes (such as training farmers or preparing teachers), were converted into schools with more extensive and more complex academic ambitions, and university departments everywhere, and of all kinds, were enthusiastically established or enlarged. Plenty of teaching jobs became available, naturally, for people with appropriate scholarly credentials.

In the discipline of philosophy as well, numerous new undergraduate and graduate departments were established, and even more numerous other departments were expanded. Thus, more students were admitted to more undergraduate and graduate philosophy programs, and more faculty members were appointed to staff the programs. The number of professionally trained and accredited philosophers in this country began very greatly to increase.

Along with these increases in the sizes of student bodies, and of faculties, and in the numbers of locations at which academic philosophy was practiced and taught, there were corresponding extensions and elaborations of what might be regarded as the infrastructure of philosophical activity. People needed to publish their work, both in order to display their wares to the world and in order to support their candidacies for promotion or for tenure. So, new philosophy journals came into existence, and new book publishing enterprises appeared.

Moreover, the notable increase in the quantity of scholarly activity, as well as the natural interest many philosophers had in establishing and maintaining personal contact with colleagues at other institutions—or the interest some philosophers had simply in traveling—these various considerations together led to a large increase in the number of academic meetings and conferences. And it led also to a large increase in the number of invitations for philosophers to present lectures at nearby or even at very distant campuses.

Needless to say, all of this large-scale creation and expansion required the expenditure of a great deal of money. The money was in fact forthcoming, but the flow of money directed to the support of higher education started rather small. For instance, my first salary, as an instructor at Ohio State University, was $4,200 a year. That now sounds pretty meager, I suppose, but at the time, it really wasn't bad at all. In fact, I found that, as a bachelor, I could live on it quite decently. Moreover, salaries generally went up at a significant rate—so that, within a very few years, I was able to take a vacation in Spain and a couple of other vacations sailing the Caribbean to the islands of Trinidad, Tobago, and Curaçao.

Since those early days, the salaries of academic philosophers—and the funding of philosophical activity in general—have continued to rise steadily and, on the whole, substantially. To be sure, there are important divisions within the academic world, and institutions of certain types—for instance, those sponsored by, or supported mainly by, religious establishments—have not been able to do nearly as well in compensating their faculties as have, for the most part, public institutions and the relatively small number of well-endowed private schools.

The same story of improvement in the condition of the profession holds true, by and large, with regard to aspects of academic employment other than salaries. Teaching loads have decreased very substantially during the period of my career and so has the availability of sabbatical time-off from teaching. Also, access to outside funding for research has been considerably expanded, with large grants and fellowships being offered by a number of relatively old as well as by a number of relatively new government agencies and private philanthropic foundations.

II

It is difficult for me to judge, with any real confidence, whether this gigantic expansion of philosophical and general university activity, and the heavily increased financial support of academic philosophers and other scholars, has been generally a good thing or on the whole a bad thing or whether perhaps it has, on the whole, actually made no real difference at all either to the overall quality of philosophical and academic life or to the cumulative value of the professional output which philosophers and other scholars have produced.

Of course, it is indisputably a good thing that many philosophers and academics of other varieties have now come to enjoy incomes that enable them to raise their families appropriately and to live comfortably without burdensome financial disabilities and anxieties. But when I learn that some people in our field are receiving salaries considerably larger than what is paid to the chief justice of the United States (about $225,000) and when I hear that some foundations are nowadays offering philosophers grants of as much as a million dollars—I begin to become bewildered and to suspect that things may be getting a little out of hand. Moreover, when I observe professional philosophers traveling rather incessantly to meetings and conferences everywhere around the world or undertaking, without much letup, to present lectures or to join in innumerable discussions or symposia, I cannot help wondering whether all that activity is truly worth the effort. To be sure, some of this running around may be beneficial—perhaps it may indeed be helpful, or even indispensable, in supporting the fundamental interests of scholarship and of personal understanding. Nonetheless, it is hard for me to avoid thinking that a great portion of it is just a waste of money and a waste of time.

III

Some of us may be reluctant to admit it, but—at least, so it seems to me—the fact is that the profession of an academic philosopher, along with the profession of academic scholars generally, has generally become a pretty good deal. Academic life used to demand sacrifices both of income and of freedom. It required a deliberate renunciation of certain benefits and advantages that other individuals, who were no more extensively educated and who were ordinarily endowed with no more than roughly comparable talents could routinely expect to enjoy. Academic life now is no longer, however, essentially a vocation or a calling. Now, it verges on being simply a career.

Salaries are quite decent, at least for many of us, and working conditions—again, at least for many of us—are excellent. We are not required to teach very much, we have long vacations, we have considerable free time even when we are not on vacation, and, at least after we have been promoted to a tenured position (if not so much, of course, before that critical transition), after it, at least, we are able to pursue our own interests, more or less at our own pace, and pretty much in whatever direction we please. Nobody looks demandingly or menacingly over our shoulders, and, on the whole, to a far greater extent than people in nearly all other professions, we run our own lives. Accordingly, as one relatively appealing career among a number of others which might plausibly be chosen, the academic profession naturally facilitates, and even encourages, the pursuit of a somewhat different way of living than it used to do.

IV

Let me turn now to recalling some of the more strictly philosophical developments that have transpired during my philosophical career (or, if you will, during my rather elongated, but only occasionally dedicated, response to my philosophical calling). When I was an undergraduate student, a large preoccupation of most of the academic philosophers with whose work I was actually acquainted—they were mostly philosophers who worked in the United States or in Great Britain—was epistemological. More specifically, these philosophers were preoccupied mainly with issues concerning perception and with the presumed access that perception offers to a reality external to and independent of ourselves. There was considerable debate over whether it was the so-called New Realists or the so-called Critical Realists who were closer to the truth about the relation of the human mind, in its perceiving, to the physical world. The Critical Realists had a dualistic understanding of the normal perceptual situation: they believed that a mentally dependent entity, a so-called sense-datum, intervenes between the perceiver and the physical object of perception that exists outside the mind. On the other hand, the New Realists adopted a monistic view, claiming that the perceiver is in touch with the outside physical object directly, without the intervention of any mental entity.

One of the most eminent Critical Realists was Professor Arthur O. Lovejoy, whose Carus Lectures, called *The Revolt against Dualism*, had set the New Realists back on their heels (at least for a while). Lovejoy was also an extremely eminent historian of ideas; in fact, together with one of my teachers at Johns Hopkins—George Boas—he founded that scholarly subdiscipline: the history of ideas. He was the author of a magisterial work in the field, entitled *The Great Chain of Being*, which is universally acknowledged to be a classic of historical and philosophical scholarship. Lovejoy was professor of philosophy emeritus at Johns Hopkins University while I was a graduate student there (i.e., from 1951 to 1954), and I had the privilege of being assigned by the philosophy department at Hopkins, during part of that time, to be his assistant.

He was then quite elderly, and his vision had deteriorated considerably. The reason he especially needed personal assistance at the time was that he was moving to a smaller apartment and needed to get rid of some of his very extensive collection of books. The titles of the books were generally too indistinctly displayed for him to read them easily. It was my special responsibility as his assistant, accordingly, to help him to identify each of the books, in order that he could decide whether to keep or to discard it. So what I did was to read to Lovejoy the title of each book as we went along the shelves and then to implement his decision whether to keep it or to throw it away—by leaving on the shelves the books which were to be kept and by placing in a separate location those which were to be discarded.

This simple process actually took quite a bit longer than might have been expected because Lovejoy insisted upon not merely indicating for each volume whether he wanted it to be discarded or to be retained but upon also recounting as we went along—often in some detail—the intellectual significance and value of each book. He was extremely erudite, so the process was sometimes interesting. On the whole, however, it was rather tedious. As a way of obtaining a little relief, Lovejoy and I would, from time to time, sit down, away from our work, and listen to radio broadcasts of baseball games. He was a fan of the Baltimore Orioles, which was at that time a minor-league team in the Triple-A International League. Lovejoy made a point of listening to broadcasts of as many Orioles games as he could, so we had numerous breaks from our work.

After I received my BA from Johns Hopkins in 1949, I spent two years as a graduate student in the Department of Philosophy at Cornell University, which was, at that time, reputed to be one of the leading philosophy departments in the country. Some of the most pioneering faculty and students then at Cornell were especially interested either in the work of Gottlob Frege or in the work of Ludwig Wittgenstein. Now, I myself, as it turned out, failed to develop a particular interest either in Frege or in Wittgenstein. I did not become especially interested in Frege because, after having become solidly convinced by some of his ideas about meaning and reference, I was nevertheless not able to see any important further philosophical uses for them. The fact that I did not become greatly interested in Wittgenstein had a different sort of explanation: it was due very largely to my having been offended by what struck me as the rather egregiously cultish aspect of the Wittgensteinian group of graduate students at Cornell.

This was at a time somewhat before Wittgenstein's *Philosophical Investigations* had been published. Norman Malcolm, who was a senior member of the Cornell faculty, had been both a devoted pupil and a friend of Wittgenstein, and as a consequence of this personal connection, there circulated among the graduate students at Cornell typewritten copies of Wittgenstein's so-called "Blue and Brown Books," which were philosophically valuable predecessors or precursors of the *Investigations*.

However, the "Blue and Brown Books" typescripts did not circulate freely. On the contrary, they were available only to a closely selected group of students. No one outside this group was permitted to see the typescripts. I felt, moreover, that the students in the select group were inclined to protect their privileged access to Wittgenstein's work in a somewhat bullying manner and that they brandished their "insiders" sophistication with a rather distastefully condescending and snobbish arrogance.

It was what seemed to me to be this cult-like behavior and attitude of theirs that effectively turned me away from developing any substantial interest in Wittgenstein. It actually (quite ludicrously, I must admit) led me to keep myself deliberately away from learning very much about his work. I regret to say—indeed, I am ashamed to say—that what I experienced as the insulting and obnoxious behavior of the Wittgensteinian clique at Cornell resulted in my preventing myself from becoming seriously conversant with what clearly was one of the most important philosophical movements of the twentieth century.

My personal experience at Cornell was not particularly either satisfying or successful, but one great thing did happen to me while I was there: I actually met Wittgenstein. He had been ill, and he was in Ithaca, recuperating at Norman Malcolm's home from some surgery. When Wittgenstein had sufficiently recovered his strength, Malcolm arranged for him to lead a discussion with the philosophy graduate students. I attended that discussion. Unfortunately, I remember essentially nothing at all about the substance of the discussion, except that it was devoted to considering the principle that "ought" implies "can" and that Wittgenstein made a great deal out of how difficult it is to arrive at a really clear understanding of what is meant by the word "can." On the other hand, although I found the substance of the discussion forgettable, the man Wittgenstein himself was quite memorably entrancing. Even apart from the subtlety and philosophical intelligence he displayed during the discussion, he shone somehow with a very remarkable, nearly incandescent, inner light—a light of single-minded and uncannily concentrated and pure dedication to a search for clarity and for truth. At least to me, it seemed that Wittgenstein was pervasively, throughout his being—almost supernaturally—dedicated to these ideals, with an unequivocal and surpassingly wholehearted commitment and integrity. I have encountered nothing like that marvelous intellectual saintliness except, perhaps, on one other occasion, when—during my undergraduate years at Johns Hopkins—I attended a lecture given by the gestalt psychologist Wolfgang Köhler.

V

In my second year at Cornell, Professor Max Black chose me to be his assistant in his graduate Introduction to Symbolic Logic course, and I also assisted Professor Gregory Vlastos in his course on the History of Political Philosophy. However, my work as a student was evidently not very successful. Indeed, although I had not been aware that my performance as a student had actually been less than satisfactory, I was informed near the end of the year that my fellowship would not be renewed. This made it financially impossible for me to return to Cornell. Accordingly, I went back to Johns Hopkins and continued my doctoral work there. After a bit more coursework—including seminars on Plato, on ethics, and on Whitehead—I wrote a doctoral dissertation entitled "The Essential Objectivity of What Is Known" and was awarded the PhD (with distinction) in 1954. A few months later, I was drafted into the army, from which I was discharged in spring 1956. (I sometimes enjoy pointing out to my colleagues at Princeton that I am the only member of our department who has been trained to kill.)

In the latter part of my service in the army, I was stationed in France. When it came time for me to plan for my return to civilian life, my location abroad made it difficult for me to look for an academic job in the United States. It was my great good fortune, however, that, while working for my doctorate at Johns Hopkins, I had become a very close friend of another graduate student there—Norman Kretzmann. After his graduation, Kretzmann had joined the faculty at Ohio State University, and while I was in France, he somehow or other managed to persuade his colleagues in the Ohio State philosophy department to offer me an appointment without the customary interview.

So I went to Ohio State. It was not, at that time, a university of especially distinguished academic standing, but, at least in a number of humanities departments, it had some very good people. During my time there, the philosophy department included several junior members who went on to notable careers—for example, besides Kretzmann himself, there were Sydney Shoemaker and Carl Ginet, the philosopher of science Dudley Shapere, and the Hegel scholar H. S. Harris, and, in addition, there was an exceptionally gifted but unfortunately quite unproductive young man named J. Sayer Minas. It was not at all a bad group.

I remained at Ohio State for six years, during which I began to develop my particular interest in the ideas of Descartes. I had become fascinated with the problem of the "Cartesian circle," and I was determined to find a way of showing that Descartes had not committed so egregious a logical blunder. I was motivated in this, apart from a perhaps naive assumption that great philosophers do not commit obvious mistakes in reasoning, by an affection for a thinker whose mind I found particularly appealing. His work attracted me especially on account of his devotion to finding an unshakeable foundation for knowledge and on account of the clarity and precision of his reasoning, and I was also attracted to research on Descartes's work by the fact that his books are short.

I left Ohio State in 1962, for a promotion and tenure at what was then the State University of New York (SUNY) at Binghamton—what is now, I believe, Binghamton University. I lasted only one year at Binghamton, which turned out to be a rather dismal place, in an extremely unappealing location. Then I was rescued, quite unexpectedly, by someone whose graduate seminar on Plato's thought I had attended at Johns Hopkins: Professor Ludwig Edelstein. Edelstein had left Hopkins for a position at the Rockefeller Institute—later, the Rockefeller University—in New York City. Rockefeller was a very remarkable academic institution, originally dedicated exclusively to advanced research in the biomedical sciences. Its president at the time was a man named Detlev Bronk, who had earlier been president of Johns Hopkins. He had known and admired Edelstein there and had persuaded him to come to Rockefeller. Bronk had recently established a program of graduate studies at Rockefeller, which had previously had no students at any level at all. It was his notion that the best scientists could not be trained in an exclusively scientific environment but that some presence of the humanities was essential. For this reason, he wanted Edelstein to create a group of philosophers who would interact with the students at Rockefeller and with the Rockefeller faculty as well, thereby (presumably) broadening everyone's perspectives and, in particular, somehow providing the scientists with a more humanistic understanding of their work.

Bronk dreamed of turning the Rockefeller Institute from purely a research institution into what he conceived would be a true university. Not only philosophers, but also physicists and mathematicians—and, in time, behavioral scientists of various kinds—were to be added to the core group of biomedical people. There were to be no undergraduates, just graduate students in the several disciplines represented on the campus. The idea was to create a rich scholarly environment in which, according to Bronk's views, it would be possible to develop genuinely deep and creative biologists.

Edelstein was quite successful personally in establishing significant relationships with a number of Rockefeller students. He was very reluctant to implement Bronk's idea of forming a group of philosophers, however, because he anticipated that the members of such a group would be strongly inclined to talk only to each other and so to have no especially productive intellectual relationships with the scientists. Thus, they would not fulfill the conception of a genuine scholarly community which Bronk and he shared. Accordingly, Edelstein agreed to bring philosophers to Rockefeller just one at a time and only as temporary visitors. I had studied Plato with Edelstein at Hopkins, he liked me, and he evidently thought I might fit in appropriately at Rockefeller. Largely as a concession to Bronk, he arranged my appointment to the Rockefeller faculty as a research associate for the year 1963–64.

Thus, I left Binghamton and moved to New York. At that time, Rockefeller was still almost exclusively a research institution, though it did already have a few graduate students in biology. The location of the institution, and its facilities, were ideal, and I was eager to remain there beyond the one year for which I had been appointed. So I made a special effort to integrate myself into the life of the campus. I attended a course designed for new graduate students who had previously not had much exposure to biological thought, and I also made a point of cultivating a few friendships with biologists, in particular with certain members of the laboratories of cell biology and of evolution (whose leading figures were, respectively, the Nobel laureate George Palade and the eminent theorist of evolution Theodosius Dobzhansky). In these ways, I became acquainted to a certain extent with advanced biological thinking. I cannot say, however, that this affected my philosophical work in any way.

It so happened that not very long after I arrived at Rockefeller, Edelstein suddenly died. Shortly after that, President Bronk called me into his office and told me that he wanted me to pursue the ambition which Edelstein had declined to carry out. He wanted me to recommend a number of philosophers for appointment and—in keeping with his intention to make Rockefeller a real university—to help in fashioning a program of graduate studies in philosophy.

As I have already indicated, Rockefeller was in many ways an extremely attractive place: it had a lovely campus on the Manhattan bank of the East River in New York City, it had no undergraduate students and no intention to have any, and it paid well. As might be expected, then, it was not terribly difficult to persuade very good people to accept positions there. Over the course of several years, a considerable number of quite well-known and distinguished philosophers joined the Rockefeller group. At one time or another, the group included Ernest Nagel, Margaret Wilson, Marshall Cohen, Joel Feinberg, Donald Davidson, Sydney Shoemaker, Robert Nozick, and others. In addition, there was a separate group of logicians, that included Hao Wang, Tony Martin, Lester Tharpe, and Saul Kripke, and, of course, there were also occasional visitors—like Willard van Orman Quine, Thomas Nagel, and Joseph Raz.

As it turned out, Edelstein was only half-right in his anxieties concerning what was likely to happen if a sizeable number of philosophers came to Rockefeller. On the one hand, it was true, as he had feared it would be, that we did not talk much to the scientists. But, on the other hand, it was also true, contrary to his expectation, that we did not talk much to each other either. We got along well enough together, but each of us tended to focus on taking personal advantage of the rare opportunity for comfortably undisturbed scholarly research and writing. And so each of us, more or less single-mindedly, went his or her own way.

For my own part, I continued to work mainly on Descartes, and late in the 1960s, I completed writing a book titled *Demons, Dreamers, and Madmen*, that dealt with what I characterized as Descartes's defense of reason. I recall that Quine was visiting Rockefeller at the time and that he advised me against giving the book that title, which he regarded as too light-hearted or frivolous for what purported to be a serious scholarly work. Needless to say, I resisted the appeal of this mature and wisely sober recommendation.

In due course, my colleagues and I did admit a few students to do graduate work in philosophy at Rockefeller. However, in keeping with what we took to be the spirit of the place, we did not concern ourselves with them very intently. They naturally expected that they had come to Rockefeller to earn advanced degrees; on the other hand, we remained rather casually indifferent to their intellectual needs. I am not at all sure now how any of them actually managed to get along under our rather presumptuous and persistent neglect. The fact is that we drove some of them crazy (I believe that we would have driven even more of them crazy, except that some of them were already crazy when they came to us). In any case, some of our students did in fact receive their doctorates, and quite a few of them have gone on to do very well: for instance, Norton Batkin, Michael Bratman, Jules Coleman, Daniel Farrell, Michael Jubien, Jonathan Lear, David Malament, and Scott Weinstein.

The Rockefeller idyll did not last. In 1976, the university decided that it was undergoing such serious financial difficulties that it could no longer afford to support the philosophers or the logicians. Now while experimental scientists—such as, research biologists—require expensively equipped laboratories, philosophers and logicians can, of course, get along quite nicely without any special facilities. However, scientists are generally supported very largely by grants from the government or from other sources outside the university. Although philosophers and logicians need very little support, they generally do have to be supported entirely from the university's own funds. So it is perhaps understandable that they may actually constitute a greater financial burden to the university than the scientists do.

In any case, we philosophers were at Rockefeller in the first place for no real reason other than to satisfy Bronk's romantic whim about creating a great center of humanistically enriched scientific education and research. The scientific faculty had not really wanted us there to begin with, and they rightly did not feel that they had benefitted much from our having been brought to the campus. Moreover, Bronk himself had died a few years earlier, and the president then current, a physicist named Frederick Seitz, had no particular commitment to Bronk's vision.

Thus, they closed us down: despite the fact that all of us were tenured, the philosophy and logic groups were disbanded and dispersed. The university made it as comfortable for us to leave as was reasonable, and all of us left—except for Hao Wang, who stayed on for a number of years until he, too, died. Apart from him, in those final days, there were five of us. Kripke went to Princeton, Martin went to UCLA, I went to Yale, Davidson went first to Illinois at Chicago and soon afterwards to Princeton, and Feinberg went to Arizona. That was the end of what I suppose was a somewhat spectacular, but not really a very successful, episode in the history of American philosophy.

VI

I loved Yale. It somehow recalled for me the scholarly environment which I had experienced as a student at Johns Hopkins and which I regarded as having been close to ideal. It was not merely that the faculties of both universities were studded with outstanding scholars. The virtues of both were not only intellectual but moral as well. On both campuses, I felt around me a dedication to scholarship, to scholarly integrity, and to a disinterested love of truth.

Another marvelous thing about Yale, not unrelated to the first, was the undergraduate student body. There had been no undergraduates at Rockefeller, which all of us on the faculty there had considered a great blessing. But at Yale, for what I think was the first time in my life, I really enjoyed undergraduate teaching. The students were not merely very intelligent. They were bright and creative, and—most important—they were genuinely interested in ideas. They came to their classes with a clear desire, not just to get good grades in order to develop impressive CVs, but to understand and to learn.

Of course, Yale had certain other peculiarities as well. When I went there, after leaving Rockefeller, I ran headlong and heedlessly into a

situation manifesting one of the most emblematic features of philosophical life in the twentieth century. I mean: the rather fraught, and sometimes overtly contentious, division between, on the one hand, what is
known as "analytic" philosophy and, on the other hand, what is known
as "Continental" philosophy. At that time, the senior members of the
Yale philosophy department were almost all devoted to Continental
philosophy, but there was one senior member of the department who
was devoted emphatically to analytic philosophy. She was rather fero-
ciously determined to see to it that the analytic mode of doing philosophy prevailed in the Yale department or that it at least became solidly
established there, and she was quite openly and belligerently contemp-
tuous of what she took to be the contrary intentions of her senior colleagues. As it happened, she had some of the junior members of the
department on her side, and so the battle was always simmering. And,
distressingly often, it raged.

I was trained as an analytic philosopher, and I identified myself quite
happily with that movement or tendency in philosophy. But I was
aware, of course, that others believed they had legitimate grievances
concerning the way of thinking which they regarded as characteristic of
analytic philosophers. The partisans of Continental philosophy generally complained that analytic philosophers tend to busy themselves, as a
matter of professional commitment, with minute technicalities of definition and argument, while ignoring more timely philosophical problems pertaining to the fundamental and perennial conflicts and perplexities of human life. On the other hand, the analytic philosophers were
inclined to complain that Continental philosophers tend to be overly
dramatic, that they pay too little attention to clarity and rigor, and that,
as a consequence, it is often extraordinarily difficult—and sometimes
not possible at all—to follow their reasoning or even to know what they
are talking about.

For my own part, I could not see any irreducibly opposed dichotomy
in this controversy. It struck me that the greatest and the most universally admired philosophical icon and paradigm—namely, Socrates—had
combined both of the two ambitions now spuriously and unnecessarily
contending: he was an analytical philosopher who devoted himself conscientiously to articulating in precise and rigorous detail the meanings
both of ordinary and of technical concepts and to designing cogent lines
of argument, and simultaneously, and exactly insofar as he was doing

that, he was concerned with exploring and illuminating the most profound and urgently problematic aspects of human experience.

I myself had for some time actually been dissatisfied with the standard analytic repertoire of philosophical issues. I did not doubt that those issues were appropriate objects of philosophical inquiry, but I believed that philosophers should devote their attentions to other issues as well. At first, I thought it would be worthwhile to explore the fact that we seek to learn about certain things not only because we crave the truth about them, but also because we find them interesting, and so it seemed to me that the concept of "interesting" was worthy of serious analytic investigation. I gave some thought to this, but I was never able to penetrate very far into the analysis of the concept. However, my effort to do so did lead somewhere: it led me to notice the concept of "what we care about."

Thus, I was led to write my essay entitled "The Importance of What We Care About," and subsequently to engage in efforts to understand the nature of the will and of the various carings and lovings that make a person's will what it is. The chief influence upon me in this undertaking was, I believe, not the work of any philosopher or philosophical group. Rather, the chief influence upon me was that of Freudian psychoanalysis, in which I had been interested since early in my undergraduate career.

I served as chairman of the Yale philosophy department for nine years. During that time—in dealing with the problems of hiring new faculty, of admitting graduate students, and of conducting other aspects of the department's affairs—I attempted to keep in mind, and to be guided by, the harmonious possibility which had been exemplified by Socrates. As it happened, shortly after I left Yale in 1990 to move to Princeton, the Yale department collapsed and spent some years in moribund receivership. I am very glad to say that it appears now to have recovered, to have repaired its wounds, and to be robustly on the way to becoming the outstanding philosophy department which Yale requires and which it deserves.

A few years after I arrived at Princeton, Yale invited me back to its faculty. I declined the invitation, but I continue to wonder whether that was the right decision. Of course, Princeton is an extremely nice place to live, and I have had excellent colleagues at the university. Moreover, I do not believe that my work would have been improved—or, indeed, affected in any way—if I had returned to Yale. At Yale, I would prob- ably have had more active relationships than at Princeton with scholars in areas such as history and literature, and I hope that I would have resumed the position I had enjoyed as a lecturer in Yale's wonderful law school. But I would doubtless have continued to function as a loner, deriving intellectual and cultural reassurance and pleasure from my environment, but not being noticeably influenced by it in my philosoph- ical work.

VII

I must confess that I know even less about what was going on in Conti- nental philosophy during my time than I know about developments among analytic philosophers. Of course, I know some of the leading Continental names: Husserl, Sartre, Gadamer, Habermas, Merleau- Ponty, Lévinas, Heidegger. And I have even tried, from time to time, to read some of their work. But I have never got very far in those attempts, and I acknowledge that I have not been really persistent enough to overcome the difficulties I have encountered in reading the texts of the leading Continental thinkers. I regret, as a matter of fact, that I have not tried harder, for I believe that I did get close enough to Continental thinking to develop a sense that there is truly something valuable in it.

I have myself tried to satisfy both the interests of Continental thought and the requirements of analytic philosophy. At least since I outgrew my early interest in epistemological problems, I have tried to deal exclusively with issues that struck me as being unmistakably of central human interest, to deal with those issues always with the great- est care for precision and clarity of expression, and to give particular attention to the necessity of being suitably rigorous in the development of my concepts and arguments. I have tended to avoid much concern with formal approaches or with elaborately technical developments. My concern has been mostly, in fact, to understand myself and my own experience of life, so I have been rather exclusively personal in my interests and in my approach.

VIII

Most of my work has been in the areas of moral psychology and the philosophy of action. I don't remember exactly how I became involved in those areas, but I do recall one pertinent incident. Some time after I finished my book on Descartes, I was one day ruminating more or less idly in my office at Rockefeller about the free-will problem, and in particular, I was turning over in my mind a certain familiar maxim, which was supposed to convey the impossibility of there being such a thing as freedom of the will. The maxim states: "A person may be able to do what he wants, but he cannot want what he wants."

It suddenly struck me, as an idea coming entirely out of the blue, that this maxim is manifestly false. It is possible for a person to want what he wants, I thought, just as it is possible that a person does not want to want what in fact he wants. This unexpected brainstorm led to my essay entitled "Freedom of the Will and the Concept of a Person" and, a bit later, to an essay promulgating the idea that in order to be morally responsible an agent need not actually have an alternative to acting as he does. What moral responsibility does require, I maintained, is just that the action which the agent performs be something which he not only has a desire to perform but that it be something which he wants more or less fully and wholeheartedly to perform—that what he does be something, in other words, which he really wants to do. This, in turn, led me to investigate the character and the various roles in human life of desire and volition. As I have already mentioned, I have been largely influenced in these investigations by Freudian thought; moreover, I have tended to pay closer attention to my own pertinent experience than to the writings of other philosophers.

I have been unable to keep up with the rather extensive scholarly literature in which discussion of my essays in moral psychology, and in the theory of action, has been carried on, and I have, on the whole, refrained from responding to the often formidably complex and intricately demanding objections which that literature has presented. The fact is that I am pretty sure my views are correct, and I suppose, I have been rather arrogantly confident that their correctness will ultimately be acknowledged without any further assistance from me. If they are actually incorrect, on the other hand, that too will in time become entirely clear regardless of what more I might say.

One reason I have tended to pay so little conscientious attention to philosophical developments during the last half-century or so is that they have often seemed too distant from familiar concepts and common experience to be of any interesting human relevance. I know I may often have been quite wrong about this. But even mathematical logic— in the elementary regions of which I was actually, at one time, somewhat decently competent—has appeared to me to be philosophically barren. I know that the claim is sometimes made that progress in mathematical logic has led to the construction of powerful instruments for the clarification and resolution of philosophical difficulties. However, I do not really know of any such instruments. Bertrand Russell's theory of definite descriptions is effective, to be sure, in untangling certain problems of reference, and the first- and second-order propositional calculi do provide occasionally useful frameworks for articulating intricate ideas unambiguously. However, it seems to me that the contribution these resources can make to important philosophical progress in my areas of interest is at best marginal.

IX

Much of the course of philosophy in recent years has been governed by immanent developments—I mean, it has been responsive directly to influences that have arisen out of the results of previous philosophical inquiry. Some of these developments have been of notable, or even of historic, philosophical importance. In the central areas of metaphysics and epistemology, the most substantial influences have been generated by the contributions of Quine and Davidson and David Lewis and by the ground-breaking innovations of Kripke. The impacts of various sorts of linguistic philosophy—from the commonsense analyses developed by G. E. Moore, to the so-called ordinary-language approach followed by certain Wittgensteinians—have been quite pervasive. Nowadays, perhaps, explicit preoccupation with linguistic theory has receded, but a particular sensitivity to the philosophical significance of linguistic structure and nuance has been commonly absorbed.

A notable feature of recent philosophical history has been the efflorescence of creative activity, among analytic philosophers, in studies of the history of philosophy and, I suppose even more conspicuously, in moral philosophy and in political theory. Much of the revival of philosophical attention to social and political issues, as well as to more general issues in ethics, has been due to the extraordinary impact made by John Rawls's book *A Theory of Justice*. This work of Rawls has given rise to an impressive secondary literature of its own, as well as to the establishment and success of at least one prestigious scholarly journal, *Philosophy and Public Affairs*.

My own contribution to issues of political theory has been limited primarily to some work criticizing the notion that economic equality is an authentic moral ideal. I argued that a concern with equality tends to encourage people to worry about how their lives compare with the lives of others and thus to divert them from attending to what they actually need in order to satisfy their own peculiar interests and in order to make their own lives good. I continue to believe that this is a valid and significant point, but my critique of the notion that economic equality is a genuine moral ideal has not attracted much support. In fact, one prominent legal theorist told me—right to my face—that he considered my view to be "despicable."

Much of what has been going on in philosophy has not been what I have referred to as "immanent development"; rather, it has been in the mode of responses to developments in other areas of thought. Certain philosophers have paid a great deal of attention, for instance, to what has been going on in the brain- and neurosciences. Much of this particular philosophical activity has been concerned with efforts to illuminate the complexities and mysteries of the mind-body problem, by trying to figure out how mental functioning is actually related to—that is, just how it is dependent upon or even, perhaps, identical with—the functioning of our brains and nervous systems, but some of the pertinent philosophical activity has been concerned with epistemological problems and some of it even with ethics.

At one time, I believed that this approach to ancient philosophical puzzles was likely to be exceptionally fruitful. In fact, I used to say that any contemporary philosopher who remained ignorant of what is going on in the brain- and neurosciences would be like a philosopher in the seventeenth century who had no idea of what was happening then in physics. I now think that this was a rather blind exaggeration.

Some of the neuroscientific material is indeed fascinating. But it is very unclear that any substantial philosophical progress has yet been built upon it or has even been convincingly promised by it. And anyhow, the comparison with seventeenth-century physics now strikes me as shallow and misconceived. Physics in the seventeenth century was not philosophically important because, as the neurosciences have certainly done and continue to do, it provided valuable new information. It was philosophically important because it generated a new conceptual repertoire and because—making use of those new concepts—it offered a new way of seeing the world. Perhaps I am missing something, but I do not believe that the brain- and neurosciences have in fact fashioned, or have even been moving in the direction of fashioning, either any comprehensive set of new fundamental concepts or any especially innovative perspective on the nature of the world or of human experience.

The emergence during the twentieth century of computers and of computer science has evoked a somewhat parallel response among philosophers. Apart from supposing that our mental activity is connected in some still unknown but philosophically important manner with the brain and the nervous system, many thinkers have found it plausible to suppose that our mental activities can best be understood as analogous to the activities of a computer. This presumptively powerful leading insight has led to a considerable flurry of interest in the design of so-called artificial intelligence, motivated by the conviction that a successful AI design would provide a useful model of how our own human minds actually work. The artificial intelligence project has had some genuine success, I believe, in dealing with such matters as voice (and even face) recognition and in robotics. But nothing of lasting philosophical significance has yet, so far as I am aware, emerged from the field.

In any case, my own efforts to become sophisticated in the pertinent scientific disciplines have been quite meager, intermittent, and unproductive. I suppose that I am still under the influence of the classic analytic dogma that philosophy is properly concerned exclusively with conceptual analysis and that for this analysis no knowledge of empirical science is necessary. As a deliberate matter, I reject this dogma. I do believe, however, that I am still gripped by it and that I am now too old to grow out of it.

A little while ago, I mentioned seventeenth-century physics. I suppose I should really say at least something about the relationship between physics and philosophy during the period of which I am speaking. Einstein and Bohr, not to mention various others, certainly made enormous changes in how science understands the world, and they certainly did not do so merely by providing us with startling new information. Of course, they did do that. But far more importantly, they also brought about fundamental changes in the conceptual scheme with which physics proposes to comprehend and to articulate the nature of things. Some philosophers have boldly confronted these changes and have attempted to develop productive philosophical responses to them. I am afraid that I can make no judgment concerning the success or even concerning the general philosophical pertinence of these attempts—indeed, I cannot even describe them—because I am simply too ignorant both of the underlying natural phenomena and of the scientific theories that focus on them.

X

Perhaps now, after having devoted my talk, so far, mainly to the recent past of philosophy, I may allow myself to speak briefly about its possible future.

I believe that there is, at least in this country, a more or less general agreement among philosophers and other scholars that our subject is currently in the doldrums. Until not very long ago, there were powerful creative impulses moving energetically through the field. There was the work in England of G. E. Moore and Bertrand Russell and of Gilbert Ryle, Paul Grice, and Herbert Hart, as well as the work of various logical positivists. In the United States, even after interest in William James and John Dewey had receded, there was lively attention to contributions by Willard Quine and Donald Davidson, John Rawls, and Saul Kripke. In addition, some philosophers were powerfully moved by the gigantic speculative edifice of Whitehead. Heidegger was having a massive impact on European philosophy, as well as on other disciplines—and not only in Europe, but here as well. And, of course, there was everywhere a vigorously appreciative and productive response to the work of Wittgenstein.

The lively impact of these impressive figures has faded. We are no longer busily preoccupied with responding to them. Except for a few contributors of somewhat less general scope, such as Habermas, no one has replaced the imposingly great figures of the recent past in providing us with contagiously inspiring direction. Nowadays, there are really no conspicuously fresh, bold, and intellectually exciting new challenges or innovations. For the most part, the field is quiet. We seem, more or less, to be marking time.

I have a fantasy about how this state of intellectual quiescence is likely to end. Of course, I have no detailed idea concerning what the creatively arousing idea or program will be. I certainly have no notion of who will bring it to us. But I do have a thought about the direction from which it will come. I think it will come, or—to backpedal just a bit—I think it is at least somewhat likely that it will come, from the direction of religion. I do not say that this will be a good thing, nor do I say that it will not be a good thing. Moreover, I cannot even pretend to be able to prove that it will happen at all. On the other hand, I can offer a few considerations that I believe lend my suggestion some support and that render it somewhat plausible.

When I was a student, practically no one would admit to having a serious intellectual interest in religion. Large numbers of my fellow students were agnostics or atheists, and many of these professed what they regarded as an enlightened disdain for religion and for religious or theological thought. Even if someone did take religion seriously as a personal matter, it was almost unheard of that such a person would recommend this attitude publicly or even display it in any way, and it was perhaps still more unheard of that someone would confess to being engaged intellectually or philosophically with religious issues.

Religion in general was simply neither practically nor theoretically respectable. Many insisted that it was not even morally respectable, and it was almost conclusively banished both from philosophical and from general academic discourse and concern. The few philosophers who did write about religious topics—they mainly reviewed arguments for or against the existence of God or puzzled over the troubling relationship between faith and reason—those few were not taken very seriously, and they were not held in very great esteem.

The situation is now quite different. Of course, philosophy of religion is still not taken very seriously, and writers on religious topics are still not held in very high academic esteem. The field is still not really respectable among the better (or, at least, among the better established) class of professional philosophers. There are, of course, some exceptions, but the number of these is still small. On the other hand, however, there has been quite a conspicuous change among students. It is not at all unusual these days for students to declare openly that they are interested in religion and that they themselves subscribe conscientiously to one or another set of religious doctrines and practices. Walking around a college or university campus these days, one sees numerous students declaring their religious attitudes and convictions quite openly: for instance, by patronizing religion-based campus institutions or by displaying some physical indicator of religious affiliation—wearing a cross, or a Star of David, or a headscarf.

Now my guess is that, at some point, at least some of these students will professionalize their interest in religion. They will articulate to themselves in more elaborate and formal detail the religious beliefs and ideas which they have earlier held less self-consciously, and they will make it their business to study those beliefs and ideas in a disciplined and scholarly way. Some of them will become—as quite a few have already become—academic students of religion and of religious thought. Some of them, in fact, will become philosophers of religion, and of these, surely, some will be significantly creative and will promulgate ideas that will provoke development and criticism by others. The game will become respectable again, and the ball will get rolling.

That is one consideration.

I have two more considerations to offer in support of my suggestion that we can expect an important creative philosophical impulse from the direction of religion. The first of these is that, over the centuries, an enormous collection has accumulated of books and monographs on topics related to theology and to the philosophy of religion. Many of those books and monographs are by authors of high intelligence and penetrating depth. Most of them have hardly ever been read. This represents a readily accessible gold mine of fresh materials for scholarly research, for courses and seminars, and for doctoral dissertations. Once the fire is lit, in other words, plenty of fuel is at hand to keep it going. Accordingly, those who are attracted to this sort of thing will easily find a great deal of suitable and stimulating work to do. This is bound to encourage bright and eager students to undertake that work, and they will move it briskly along.

My final point in this connection is that, as a matter of fact, academic moral philosophy has itself actually been moving lately in the direction of religious thought. Moral philosophers have taken up certain fundamental human problems that have characteristically been especially within the province of religious inquiry and discussion: for instance, issues having to do with the nature of virtue and with the meaning of life. It is partly with issues of this variety—and with related issues concerning the nature of sin, or of holiness, or of being sacred, or of salvation—that I would expect the philosophy of religion to be again, in coming years, largely concerned.

We philosophers have, so far, hardly any understanding of certain concepts that are quite central not only to specifically religious experience but also to human life in a more general aspect. For instance, we have no lucid and sufficient grasp of the very notion of spirituality itself. What actually is the spiritual aspect of human life, what is a spiritual guide supposed to be guiding us about, what exactly are spiritual needs and spiritual interests? What does it mean for a person to be spiritual?

It is topics like these that await serious philosophical investigation and that are likely, I suspect, to arouse significant creative attention.

But, of course, who knows? Needless to say, it is entirely possible that I have got the future quite wrong, just as I have in fact been quite wrong about much of what has happened in the past. I don't really have a great deal of confidence in my anticipation of how philosophy is likely to develop, any more than I have much confidence in my judgments concerning how philosophy has been developing, in recent years, right before my eyes.

Anyhow: there you are.

NOTE

John Dewey Lecture delivered before the 107th annual Eastern Division Meeting of the American Philosophical Association in Boston, Massachusetts, on December 29, 2010. Used by permission of the John Dewey Foundation.

7

GOD AND EVIL AMONG THE PHILOSOPHERS

Marilyn McCord Adams

I. BEGINNINGS

My questions have always revolved around God and evil. My Bible-Belt upbringing had seemed to afford vivid and convincing acquaintance with each and both. My deep-felt but then imperfectly articulated issues were these: Why would God create people only to permit them not merely to make miserable but seemingly to ruin one another's lives by relentlessly and systematically trying to destroy one another's sense of self-worth or purpose? Why would God imbed human personalities in biochemistry that could imprison them with muscular dystrophy or twist and warp them with clinical depression or schizophrenia? Why would God make persons developmental for so long, deeply impressionable and highly vulnerable to the adults who control their lives? Why would God make human beings capable of forging deep and wholesome personal connections, only to rip them apart in death? Whatever God's reasons for making us in this world, why is God so elusive? Is God like a seducer who inspires confidence, only to abandon and betray trust? Certainly, I was not worried by small to medium-sized evils that stimulate the problem solving that gives zest to life or even large-sized evils that one can learn to work around. My concern was with evils that press people up against their limits and exceed their coping powers.

By high school, my sense of anger within and evil without eclipsed any conscious experience of the reality of God. I couldn't believe any more. In Bible-Belt fashion, I reckoned that if God existed and faith was a gift, the promises of God must not be true for me. Since it was so easy, I independently discovered many of the puzzle objections to theism and biblical narratives that filled the philosophy of religion articles of the fifties and sixties. I also reasoned, in truly sophomoric fashion, that meaning was to be sought at the heart of reality. In a world without God, nuclear physics must be the ticket. In 1961, I enrolled in engineering physics at the University of Illinois, Champaign-Urbana. I soon discovered that physics courses were not about metaphysics and meaning but inclined planes and problem sets. The teachers rejected my questions as "philosophical."

So I switched majors at the end of my first year. It took another year of "hanging out" at various campus ministries before my emotional static cleared and my sense of the reality of God returned. But reacquaintance with the reality only renewed my questions. I spent hours in the YMCA reading Kierkegaard and existentialist theologians. Bill Wainwright introduced me to analytic philosophy of religion and quietly modeled what it is to be a Christian philosopher. A 1963 summer reading course on the problem of evil with Nelson Pike sent me off in the fall of 1964 to graduate school at Cornell.

II. MISFIT WITH MORALS?

Moral philosophy traffics in good and evil. So it might seem an obvious place for someone with my questions to begin. For better or worse, I was "turned off" by philosophical ethics right from the start. At the University of Illinois, Bill Diggs began his history of ethics course with Aristotle. He then announced that the Middle Ages was the most interesting period in the history of ethics, but that we would not be allowed to discuss it unless and until we could prove the existence of God to all rational people. Certainly, as an undergraduate, I lacked the philosophical skill needed to formulate Richard Swinburne's or Bill Alston's later arguments for the existence of God from religious experience. Diggs proceeded to leapfrog to Hobbes, Hume, Kant, and Mill.

Diggs's course on rule utilitarianism represented morality as a system of rules to obey the social rules and so to maintain a stable social frame. But—unadjusted for justice issues as the 1964 readings seemed to be—I couldn't see how rule utilitarianism would touch the problems of child abuse from which I started. Societies oversimplify: peace and tranquility seem more easily achieved by not acknowledging systemic evils. Moreover, the taboos erected to make certain behaviors unthinkable also sweep their actual violations under the rug. Social mores often count abusers and oppressors as model citizens and leaders, as people above reproach. "Rules to obey the rules" seemed to turn morality into status quo maintenance and to make it complicit in the very evils that troubled me the most.

I resonated with Plato's picture of moral education, with its privileging of intellectual ability and skill and its aim at reunion with a transcendent Good, until Aristotle's more realistic estimate sounded the verdict: there is no hope of becoming virtuous for the badly brought up. Neither did exposure to Kant's noumenal freedom do anything to shake my conviction that morality bears down with oughts with which not everyone is psychologically able to comply.

Certainly, my youthful early sixties encounters did not bring me to any sophisticated grasp of the moral theories we studied. Certainly, many outstanding philosophers have given moral philosophy a much more thorough, rigorous, and diversified development in the meantime. All the same, I don't think I was wrong to sense that the field was not focused in ways that would illuminate my problem. Reflecting on it now, I might try to relocate the misfit this way. John Rawls's *A Theory of Justice* is concerned with ideals of justice; questions about how to deal with stubbornly nonideal conditions are left for later discussion. Reinhold Niebuhr, pragmatist par excellence, was focused on how to avoid the worst and how far from the worst we can get in society as we know it. Susan Wolf rivets attention on personal morality and argues that morality is overrated because—in the lives of good and decent people—there are other positive values (such as loves) that can and in some sense should compete successfully with moral demands. My concern accentuates the negative: there are evils that are too bad for morality to manage (I call them "horrors"). My question is: what if anything can be done now that the worst has already happened to secure positive meaning in horror-participants' lives?

My last semester as an undergraduate, the philosophy department joined forces with math to defeat a proposal to establish a religion department at the University of Illinois. When I got hold of the flyer with their embarrassingly bad arguments, I marched into the chair's office to protest. With a patronizing smile, he explained that they didn't have to be good arguments; they were meant to persuade. What would Plato have said? This was the first crack in my naïveté about professional philosophy.

III. THE SAGE SCHOOL OF PHILOSOPHY

To accept admission to the mid-sixties Sage School was to sign on for boot camp in philosophical analysis. With three four-page papers and one twenty-five-page paper per course and three courses per semester, they drilled us in the skills of distinction drawing and concision. An essay that spilled a few lines beyond the fourth page would come back with "this paper is too long!" "Say it once, say it clearly and precisely, and quit!" "If you can make one point well, perhaps you can move on to several." The program proved very effective in getting these lessons across. Only later did I discover that these skills are not common to all academics. Certainly, I am very grateful for that training. During my twenty-one years at UCLA, razor-sharp analytical precision was a central shared value. To this day, it does my heart good to watch our graduates exhibit it in their own work.

Nevertheless, then as now, now as then, God and evil were my questions. And, despite Pike's presence, the mid-sixties Cornell philosophy department was not a particularly apt place to pursue them. Norman Malcolm dominated the scene. Max Black was also around, although by then he was not putting much effort into his teaching. Oxbridge was their Mecca and Medina. The department found funds to underwrite a semester's visit for one don per year—Paul Grice, Timothy Smiley, shorter stints from Philippa Foot and cigar-wielding, leather-jacket wearing Elizabeth Anscombe herself. The prevailing ideology (and I use that term advisedly) was a (for me bewildering) mixture of the later Wittgenstein and various strands of ordinary-language philosophy, with nods to Frege, Russell, and Moore. There was no need for foreign or formal languages. I was told to quit wasting time learning

Greek. Logic consisted of Quine's *Methods* sans proofs and footnotes plus several weeks of pre-new-theory-of-reference morning star and evening star. Sprachgefühl, an ear for usage, was what was required. Linguistic and conceptual analysis ruled the day.

In the mid-sixties, the Sage School of Philosophy was rife with doctrines, mostly rooted in various forms of verificationism and unacknowledged antirealism. Metaphysics was declared to be the study of philosophical methodology. No special courses in metaphysics needed to be offered because method was taught in every course! Necessary being was impossible. The notion of real essences or natural kinds was unintelligible, likewise any non-reductive idea of causal powers or causally necessary connections. Perhaps oddly, in those days at Cornell, analyticity survived. Skepticism was dismissed as a philosophical confusion, a fly whose way out of the bottle Wittgenstein had shown. The correct answer to the question "Can I know that I am in pain?" was "no" because one can know only that about which it is conceptually possible to be mistaken!

History was taught to the Oxbridge syllabus: Plato and Aristotle, Descartes, Leibniz, Locke, Berkeley, and Hume. We were encouraged to read the texts of past masters as if they were articles in *Mind* or *Analysis*. Malcolm's history of philosophy of mind course was a review of past mistakes. When I pointed out how Jaakko Hintikka had misinterpreted Descartes, Malcolm replied, "Who cares? He has such an interesting idea!" David Sachs's course on Plato's *Sophist* did not get beyond eight Stephanus pages. With the exception of Richard Sorabji's courses on Aristotle, we were encouraged to read piecemeal and anachronistically. Like method, Locke, Berkeley, and Hume surfaced repeatedly. Kant was taught for the first time in years during my last semester of courses and then only because of Strawson's "discovery" that Kant was a precursor of Wittgenstein.

My problems with the program were legion. The short explanation is that I simply couldn't credit many of the dogmas that the mid-sixties Sage School purveyed.

Wittgensteinian Biases

First, there was the closeted antirealism. Malcolm presented the later Wittgenstein as a philosophical messiah without roots or lineage. To me, the *Philosophical Investigations* and the "Blue and Brown Books" read more like a series of aphorisms than works of philosophy. His project was not set in the context of the Wiener Kreis. Attempts to classify or characterize his moves as, say, akin to behaviorism in the philosophy of mind or as a version of Carnapian antirealism, were rejected as idiotic incomprehensions. Wittgenstein came to bring an end to philosophy. Attempts to locate him in the history of philosophy would demonstrate how one had really not understood at all. My own puzzlement found relief when Robert Coburn assigned the Rush Rhees Wittgensteinian D. Z. Phillips's book *The Concept of Prayer*.[1] Phillips was explicit: Wittgenstein was an antirealist. There was no such thing as Reality with a capital *R* over and against which language games could be measured for veridicality. What counted as reality was language-game relative. Philosophy should leave things just as they are. If a language game is played, let it be played!

For me, antirealism has always been a nonstarter. Vivid experience convinced me of what it cannot prove: that God is a Reality that transcends human linguistic practices, relative to later jargon, a Reality "too big" to be socially constructed. I saw Phillips's book as constituting an elegant reduction of the Wittgensteinian program as he saw it. Religious-language games are played. But many religious-language games are metaphysical. In Christianity, one has only to think of the Nicene Creed or the Chalcedonian definition in Christology. Yet, metaphysics is *ganz verboten*. Apparently, philosophy does not leave everything as it is!

Phillips and, in my later experience, Rogers Albritton emphasized that religious-language games are distinct from ordinary-language games and urged that many puzzles and questions result from the illegitimate transfer of usage from the ordinary-language games of minds and persons to religious-language games. Yet, both Phillips and Albritton imported ordinary-language-game sensibilities to insist that it was a confusion to think of God as a disembodied mind who can intervene in our world to do one thing rather than another. Albritton denied that Christians really held this, while Phillips distinguished "deep" from "superstitious" religion. But I myself was a Christian, who believed, and knew of many others (not least, Anselm, Aquinas, Scotus, and Ockham) who believed, God to be an immaterial person (or immaterial persons à la the doctrine of the Trinity) who can intervene in our world. Otherwise, I didn't see how my problems with evil could have any solution. When evils are many and horrendous, there had better be some suprahuman agency that is able and eventually willing to clean up the mess! Even then, I had enough intellectual self-confidence to refuse the charge of shallowness as a piece of ad hominem abuse.

IV. THE DOGMAS OF EMPIRICISM

Turning away from the later Wittgenstein, I found that other Cornellian dogmas also made hash of attempts to understand philosophical theology. The God of patristic and medieval theology is the ultimate explainer who is supposed to exist necessarily. But—even on Fregean assumptions—only numbers and semantic intensions were allowed to exist necessarily. Where causally interactive beings are concerned, all real existence is contingent! In patristic and medieval theology, the Divine essence is supposed to be a real essence that belongs to the individual(s) to whom it belongs essentially. But only nominal essences were permitted, and de re necessities were disallowed. When I arrived at Cornell in 1964, Pike was likening the term "God" to title terms like "President of the United States." My very first article used this machinery to argue that the existence of God is not a hard fact—an idea that traditional theology would find ridiculous.

Such empiricist dogmas shaped the way the problem of evil was formulated at the time. J. L. Mackie's 1955 article "Evil and Omnipotence"[2] mounted an "atheological" argument that the existence of evil is logically incompatible with the existence of an omniscient, omnipotent, and perfectly good God. For medieval theologians, God's not existing, God's lacking one or more perfections were metaphysical impossibilities. For them, problems of evil broke into two: metaphysical difficulties about the ontological status of evil, given the metaphysical doctrine that "good" and "being" convert and soteriological questions about how and to what extent God makes good on the evils that created persons do and suffer in their lives. My own concerns lay closer to the second.

Because the God that Mackie didn't believe in was supposed to be personal, Mackie construed perfect goodness in terms of moral goodness and insisted that a morally perfect being would want to prevent or eliminate all of the evil that it could. The response that we ordinarily excuse people on grounds of weakness or ignorance did not seem to help where an omnipotent and omniscient God was concerned. The background consensus against real essences or natural kinds kept theists from even considering what traditional theology took for granted: viz., that the Divine essence itself is an immeasurable good, appropriate relation to which would be immeasurably good for human persons. This meant that—in responding to Mackie—theists agreed to work with the packages of valuables recognized by unbelievers and to suggest that these were the greater goods in the interest of which even an omnipotent and omniscient God might not prevent or eliminate evils. This led them to formulate "best of all possible worlds" and "free will" defenses at a high level of abstraction that kept the ghastliness of real evils (the ones I call "horrors") out of plain view.

V. SURVIVAL STRATEGY

Ideologically at odds with the powers-that-were, I was in urgent need of a strategy for negotiating the program without perjury. Happily, Pike suggested a way forward with his conception of philosophy of religion. Pike carved out a place for this subfield by insisting that philosophy of religion was not about making theological assertions. Rather, it was a meta-discipline, whose task was to analyze the concepts and assess the arguments used by theologians practicing within a given religious tradition. The project was first and foremost analytical. Here (as noted above) the mid-sixties Sage School was a real help. Second, Pike emphasized, philosophy of religion cuts across every area of philosophy (e.g., philosophy of mind, epistemology, ethics) so that the philosopher of religion must be "a generalist" with sufficient competence in them all. Third, as a meta-discipline, philosophy of religion presupposed familiarity with the theological materials it was analyzing. In working through a problem, Pike was adroit in selecting key points from prominent past figures. Anselm and Aquinas were called in to analyze the concept of omnipotence. Boethius was adduced to formulate the foreknowledge problem and was brought forward again for a move in its solution. Maimonides and Aquinas were used to raise and chart moves towards solving the problem of attribution. In Pike's usage, figures weren't examined in detail for their own sake, but neither were they brought up simply to trash their positions as silly. Pike spent time on them only if they offered a promising move or made an instructive mistake. He was too serious about philosophy for one-upsmanship games.

The concept of meta-discipline caught my attention. In Cornell courses on philosophy and mind and action-theory, why not treat the assignments as occasions to analyze what Hume had to say about a given topic and perhaps what Wittgenstein or some other favored contemporary would say in response? That would save me from risking and/or undertaking to defend substantive positions that might run afoul of prevailing philosophical winds. For the twelve courses that I took, five or six of my term papers were on Hume's *Treatise*. I followed the same strategy when it came to my dissertation. I had considered trying to develop an argument for the existence of God from religious experience. But in the mid-sixties Sage School, epistemology and philosophy of mind were much too vexed. Pike's then-current interest was the foreknowledge problem.[3] So I decided on a meta-thesis that would survey and analyze what medieval authors said about that. I had aimed to be comprehensive, but when my treatments of Boethius and Ockham swelled to three hundred pages, I decided to file the dissertation.

"Dogmatism" is a harsh but accurate term for what I experienced at Cornell. To challenge or ask for reasons—as I occasionally did—risked public humiliation, at its mildest an "Oh, I would have thought that obvious." Semantic put-downs—"that makes no clear sense"—were the "short way" of choice. They seemed to conspire to render the problems I really cared about unspeakable. We all know how very hard it is to rebut charges of semantic vacuity when you're in no position to ignore them! I saw stacks of papers returned, some (not mine) marked "C" (the failing grade for graduate students) because they had stepped out of ideological line. Sachs wanted to flunk my thesis on Divine foreknowledge and free will on the ground that it is a pseudo-problem, resting on metaphysical assumptions, which Albritton had shown to be picture thinking devoid of cognitive content. I got off with a sixty-page appendix and a warning that such work was "an ill omen for my career."

My three years in the Sage School convinced me that dogma is not a content but a modality, a way of holding beliefs that enforces them on others. Certainly, some forms of Bible-Belt religion are dogmatic. But it is possible to be just as dogmatic about philosophical contentions and method. The problem is that dogmatism is a sin against philosophy. In my courses, I have endeavored to put up a hedge against it—by making sure to include many points of view on each topic and by trying to convey to students that our business is not to agree, but to understand a variety of approaches and to practice analytical skills that they will need for developing their own thoughts. On the bright side, Cornell was where I met and married fellow student and sparring partner, Robert Merrihew Adams, whose wide-ranging interests eventually weighted ethics, metaphysics, and modern classical philosophy. Much later, we had to laugh when I spent our sabbatical year writing about horrendous evil, while Bob finished his magnum opus, *Finite and Infinite Goods*.[4] Like Jack Sprat and his wife, we figured, we had licked the value platter clean!

VI. HISTORY OF PHILOSOPHY AS A DISCIPLINE

Because my questions were about God and evil, because I was trying to become a philosopher of religion, ducking into the history of philosophy was not simply a cowardly survival strategy in a hostile intellectual environment. Medieval philosophical theologians were the ones who discussed the ideas and problems I was interested in with rigor and philosophical backbone. On Pike's conception, the analytical task of the philosopher of religion required fine-grained familiarity with what they said. So I determined to dig right in.

The Historical Turn

In the spirit of those times, Pike's engagement with medieval thinkers tended to be piecemeal: when analyzing an attribute of God (say, omnipotence), look at what Augustine, Anselm, Aquinas, or Schleiermacher have to say about omnipotence. His own attempts to read them as ordinary-language philosophers resulted in anachronisms that left swatches of relevant text unaccountable (e.g., why would anyone say, God is God's wisdom?). I couldn't accept what others of my teachers suggested: that such utterances were simply meaningless. Already a rebel and something of a sleuth, I decided to make it my project to get inside these thinkers to figure out what they really meant to say and why. Certainly, medieval scholastics were analytic philosophers: they were distinction-drawers and argument-inventers par excellence. But they were not only generalists (ranging over all of the major subfields of philosophy) in the way Pike recommended, they were systematic philosophers. To get a grip on what they were saying about omniscience or omnipotence or perfect goodness required a wider understanding of their metaphysics and epistemology, their conceptions of agency and normative grounds, and of how they fitted these together.

Working on my Ockham book,[5] I became convinced that their theological disagreements were rooted in philosophical differences, which were at bottom contentious. Most of their arguments for their own and against their opponent's positions involved premises to which the other would not consent. Although they were as interested as Pike was in analyzing whether Divine foreknowledge is incompatible with free will, they did not see themselves engaged in a meta-discipline but in theory construction. They were beginning with doctrinal givens and philosophical commitments and working in different ways to integrate these into a philosophically coherent system. Their debates forced refinements in their own theories. Together, they furnished detailed maps of theoretical alternatives.

Throughout my studies of medieval philosophical theology, I have remained a metaphysical realist about philosophical claims: there is such a thing as Reality with a capital R, and well-formed theories either do or do not correspond with it. But refereeing their philosophical disputes, I became a skeptical realist, holding that it is impossible for us to prove, in a way convincing to every rational person, which theory is true and which false. The philosophical task ought to concentrate on theoretical development and understanding.

It also struck me that scholastic method was an antidote for dogmatism. True, there were theological givens that medieval scholastics had to number among the phenomena to be saved. But questioning and disputing required each to get inside the other's theory enough to understand its strengths and weaknesses, the better to appreciate the pluses and minuses of their own. Such exercises foster intellectual flexibility and imagination that is able to do comparative anatomy and cost-benefit analyses on philosophical competitors and to recognize that the same problem can be solved in different ways. When, over the years, colleagues and graduate students have murmured that history of philosophy isn't really philosophy, my contrary reply has become that history of philosophy is a way of doing philosophy and wholesome medicine against the dogmatism that sometimes plagues our field.

In my generation, we by and large changed the way history of philosophy is done by philosophers trained in the analytic tradition. There is a spectrum of practice. Some do philology and edit texts. More spend time on the institutional settings and wider intellectual milieu in which past philosophers worked. There are those who focus more on the interpretive and philosophical problems found in the texts themselves, while others move on from this to build bridges to contemporary thought. All of these are important. Whatever one's specialty, one has to learn from them all. My own work on Ockham benefitted enormously from the generosity of the editorial team at the Franciscan Institute, where critical texts of Ockham's works, discoveries and perspectives, and hospitality were shared. Anachronism and misreadings are to some extent inevitable. My own advice is to resist attempts to take the weirdness out of great past philosophers. Letting them be as weird as they are is the way to guarantee that we learn something that we didn't know before.

Anglo-American analytic philosophy borrowed its sense of the philosophical canon from Oxbridge: ancient and modern classical, at least Plato and Aristotle, at least Descartes, maybe Leibniz, certainly Locke, Berkeley, and Hume. During the seventies and eighties, Kant was reentering the mainstream. Medieval philosophy has been central to the canon of philosophy in Roman Catholic schools since 1880 when Pope Leo XIII declared Aquinas the patron of the Catholic schools. Fortunately for me, a tradition of covering medieval philosophy had begun at UCLA when Ernest Moody, the famous pioneer in the study of medieval logic, joined the philosophy faculty in the late fifties and helped launch the Center for Medieval and Renaissance Studies. In leading analytic graduate departments, however, medievalists were and still are rare.

My generation failed to secure a place for medieval philosophy within the canon of analytic philosophy but not for want of trying. In the late seventies, the quality of medieval sessions at the APA had sunk so low that we specialists formed the Society for Medieval and Renaissance Philosophy, which has since mounted its own double sessions (one on the Latin West and the other on Jewish and Arabic philosophy) at divisional meetings. This was good advertising: the Middle Ages was too a period during which real philosophy was done! The society also built bridges between secular non-Catholic and Roman Catholic schools and widened the circle around which work was shared. These were significant fruits. Certainly, I have learned a lot about Aquinas from Catholic neo-Thomists, who have spent their adult lives steeping themselves in his works. Over the course of my career, more and more works have been edited and translated with the result that most professionals now know: Augustine and Aquinas were not the only philosophers between Aristotle and Descartes! But medieval philosophy is every bit as technical as contemporary metaphysics is. I suspect many think it would be too much trouble to master it. More's the pity because medieval philosophy is full of distinctive insights and theories in metaphysics, ethics, philosophy of language, and philosophical theology, overall a fascinating diet of contrasting ideas.

VII. ANALYTIC PHILOSOPHY RECONCEIVED

Studying medieval philosophy not only acquainted me with content to analyze, it gradually brought about an imitative shift in my own method. Medieval philosophical theologians were not practicing a meta-discipline; they were involved in theory construction. By the early to mid-seventies, however, analytic philosophy was recovering its sense of vocation to theorize as well. Hilary Putnam revived talk of natural kinds. Saul Kripke made *de re* necessities and mind-body dualism respectable. David Lewis's clear and penetrating discussions lent further credibility to the enterprise of metaphysics. Philosophy of mind went interdisciplinary with the rise of cognitive psychology and diversified with many and various materialist theories of the mind. Philosophy of language forged ties with linguistics. Enriched conceptual machinery from the present and retrievals from the past made it increasingly natural for me to see the project of philosophy of religion in terms of theory-construction, of articulating theological claims using philosophical conceptuality, of arguing for them—at least in part—on philosophical grounds, of adjusting concepts and theses to achieve theoretical coherence. Such a shift blurs the boundaries between philosophy of religion and philosophical theology. In fact, my own methodological turns were part of a trend that spawned a significant movement: the Society of Christian Philosophers.

VIII. GOD AMONG THE PHILOSOPHERS

For some decades before I entered philosophy, philosophy of religion had been encumbered with unreasonable burdens of proof. Diggs had not been original in warning, "Don't bring God into philosophical theory unless and until you can prove the existence of God to all corners." There was no willingness to weigh up the theoretical advantages to be won, to consider the range of theoretical jobs that might be covered simply by including God among a theory's ontological posits. When I pointed out to one famous historian of philosophy how Divine ideas serve the same function as abstract objects or Platonic forms, she was dismissive: "I like to think that modern classical philosophers were interested in real problems," she said. Likewise, in the heady days of the later Wittgenstein, philosophers of religion were warned off any discussion of the resurrection or immortality, unless and until the notion of disembodied persons could be shown to be intelligible.

By the late seventies, Christian philosophers were frankly tired of this. In the summer of 1978, Bob and I received a letter inviting us to join with other senior Christian philosophers to organize what became the Society of Christian Philosophers. Its purpose was to create space for the unfettered exploration of the wider syllabus of philosophy of religion and philosophical theology. Because the society was not meant to be a church, it had no stake in enforcing doctrinal conformity. Any who self-identified as philosophers and Christians were and are welcome to join. From the beginning, the society was extremely successful. It fostered Alston's work on religious experience,[6] the Reformed epistemology movement culminating in Plantinga's magnum opus trilogy on warrant,[7] renewed interest in postmortem destinies, as well as fresh approaches to the problem of evil and religious ethics, among others from the Adams clan. The society's activities quickly expanded beyond APA sessions to regional meetings organized to give Christian philosophers more opportunities to present their work and to receive constructive feedback. Likewise, in launching our journal, *Faith and Philosophy*, we also committed ourselves to furnish comments on articles, whether or not they were deemed suitable for eventual publication.

Meanwhile, across the ocean, John Hick had been laboring since the early sixties on major issues in philosophy of religion—faith and reason, the problem of evil, death and eternal life, religious pluralism. Apart from the ideals of rigor and clarity, Hick moved ahead mostly unfazed by the more infelicitous biases of Oxbridge analysis. Already in the seventies, Richard Swinburne was adding momentum, launching his important series of books with *The Concept of Miracle*,[8] *The Coherence of Theism*,[9] and *The Existence of God*.[10] These transatlantic philosophers made it easier for the society to forge links with philosophers of religion in the UK and Europe. More recently, the society has established connections with Chinese Christian philosophers, organized meetings involving Russian philosophers and Russian Orthodox theologians, and sent delegations to Iran to participate in philosophical conferences on religious pluralism, among other issues. Now in its thirty-third year, the society continues to flourish and is the largest special-interest group associated with the APA.

When Nick Wolterstorff and I both found ourselves at Yale Divinity School fifteen years later, we built up a program in philosophical theology and philosophy of religion, which insisted on cross-fertilization. In our "considered" opinion, theologians would do well to recognize philosophy as the backbone of theology. If they hoped to profit from the medievals, they had better learn some Plato and Aristotle. If they wanted to deal responsibly with twentieth-century German theologians, they needed to hike down the hill and take courses on Kant and Hegel! Philosophers of religion were counseled that if they wanted to know what they were talking about, they needed to learn at least as much theology as well-educated clergy did. We taught many wonderful students who took our advice with varying degrees of seriousness. For the ten years it lasted, the education we offered did much to increase the rigor and texture of both fields.

IX. WIDENED DATA BASE

Medieval philosophical theology is a rich resource for contemporary philosophy of religion. But God and evil were my questions, and knowing a chunk of the theological tradition was not enough by itself. When Pike spoke of the materials whose concepts and arguments he meant to analyze, he restricted his attention to theologians who focus (as he put it) on "the belief element" in religion. Yet, surely to theorize about the God of biblical religion, it is necessary to study the Bible itself. Likewise, if God and evil were my questions, my focus was on horrors, evils that were prima facie ruinous for human persons, insofar as participation in them seems to destroy the possibility of making positive sense of their lives. Surely, a deeper appreciation of human psychology was needed. And so, in the summers and falls of '83 and '84, I went off to Princeton Theological Seminary to fill in these gaps.

Neglected Values

Because the Bible is the primary authority within the Christian religion, believers want to get as much out of it as possible. To that end, scholars have borrowed, invented, and deployed many interpretive strategies. By the time I got to Princeton, source criticism (which divides the texts into bits derived from different traditions), form criticism (which recognizes distinctive types of structured units with distinctive functions), and redaction criticism (which looks to the distinctive ways different books weave the pieces together) were taken for granted. Literary criticism was "all the rage" and was being applied to bring out previously ignored features of narratives. The latest emphasis appealed to social anthropology. Biblical materials reflect 1,700 years of Middle Eastern culture. The societies of Abraham or Joshua or David or Jesus or Saul of Tarsus were very different from our own. Because theology "maps up" social models to characterize God-creature relations, it is important to get the background social arrangements right.

As a medievalist, I had become a text-person and so was well positioned to learn much from all of these methods, much that was pertinent to my questions about God and evil. Especially helpful were the readings in social anthropology, which made it clear how human societies have conceptualized the evaluation of human behavior in different and noncongruent ways. The Bible does not structure relations between Divine and human agents according to the categories of modern moralities. It does not, for instance, anticipate Allen Wood's Kant in representing God as one rational autonomous agent among others, living together in peace and harmony in the kingdom of ends, each and all following the categorical imperative. The dominant biblical calculus is the honor code,[11] which focuses not on actions or states of affairs but on the sacred worth of persons. Patrons have no obligation to take on clients. Rather, not doing so would be shameful because it would send the message that there was not as much to them as everyone thought. Moreover, a patron's honor is invested in his clients, whose welfare and loyalty measure how worthy a patron he is. Abandonment or neglect in time of need seems to show that the patron is weak or un-resourceful or simply doesn't care. Failure of follow-through on projects or pledges signals a lack of personal integrity, that the patron lacks wisdom to start only what he can finish, power and resolve to finish what he starts. The Bible's God is patron-king—the people of God, mostly worthless clients. To uphold Divine honor, God has to make good on the project anyway. The Exodus story shows God coming to the rescue just in the nick of time. The Christian resurrection story advertises God as someone resourceful enough to make good on a situation after the worst has already happened, after it is already too late. Such plots held out some promise, where my problems with God and evil were concerned.

Likewise, the honor code and the purity and defilement calculus[12] seemed to me to do a better job of conceptualizing what is so bad about horrors. Horror-participation does not invariably involve anything morally wrong (e.g., mind-twisting schizophrenia or accidental traumas do not). Even when it does (as with the Nazis in Auschwitz), it seems anemic to say that Hitler is guilty of moral wrongdoing. Horrors violate the sacred worth of a person. They shatter core integrity so that the person is not able to put Humpty Dumpty back together again. Alternatively, where purity is being wholly and completely of a given kind and dirt is stuff out of order, horror participation defiles by rendering persons dysfunctional seemingly beyond human powers to repair. If meaning-making is an essential function of persons, both the honor code and the purity and defilement calculus capture the degradation involved in being plunged below human norms by becoming functionally incapacitated.

Remodeled Agency

Scotus found incompatibilist freedom empirically obvious. For most adherents, incompatibilist freedom is a theoretical posit, on the one hand a condition of the possibility of moral accountability and on the other of there being agents other than God robust enough to blame for the origin of evil. My problem, however, targeted evils with power to wreck and ruin human agency, to stalemate its efforts to make positive sense of life. My seminary studies in developmental psychology, as well as readings in psychoanalytic authors such as Freud and Jung, acquainted me with a variety of models of the functional dynamics and consequent fragility of the human person. Without wholly buying into any particular theory, I found these accounts far more realistic than the idealized agencies of philosophical ethics and some theologies. These studies in psychology proved conceptually expansive and enriched my efforts to understand human personality, its meaning-making functions, and its relation to God.

X. ROOTING IN EXPERIENCE

Some philosophical problems are more abstract than others. Perhaps proving Fermat's last theorem depended only on mathematical genius and had nothing to do with Wiles's personal relations or wider culture. But it would be foolish to try to do aesthetics without a deep appreciation of one or more art forms. Computational cleverness without moral sensitivity leaves ethics wooden. Pop psychology will tell you both that many are drawn to problems of evil by their own experience of evil and that theorizing about it is easily distorted if the "Job within" is pushed too far underground. Personally, I wasn't ready to face what I really thought about the problem of evil until my midlife crisis forced me to pause and get to know myself better. Of equal importance was confronting horrendous evil again at close range. I was working in a Hollywood parish during the AIDS epidemic in the early eighties and attempting to preach to the dying and to their friends and lovers whose social worlds were dying. The urgency of their suffering, panic, and confusion cut through my cautions and inhibitions and forced me to begin to blurt out what I had to say.

XI. THE MOVE TO THEOLOGY

I didn't actually write my two books on God and evil[13] until I had moved from philosophy departments into theology. Over the course of my career, conceptions of analytic philosophy had transmogrified: once again, from the mid-sixties Sage School's focus on language analysis that held itself aloof from other disciplines to recognition that analysis presupposed familiarity with what was being analyzed (philosophy of science, with science; aesthetics, with art; philosophy of religion, with religion) to efforts at theory construction that benefitted from cross-disciplinary exchange. The unsurprising result was that some of us became straddlers. What gets taken for granted and what gets problematized, what looms large as a compelling preoccupation and what can be safely ignored, varies from field to field. Moving into theology, I felt finally freed both from the old "atheological" burdens of proof and from the hovering contempt for history of philosophy. I was stimulated by new questions and fresh connections. My sixteen years in theology faculties were very fruitful academically and opened surprising opportunities for public leadership in LGBT causes. One result of living in two worlds was that colleagues on both sides didn't (and perhaps still don't) know what to make of me. As the professor who introduced my first Gifford lecture wryly commented, "Looking over Professor Adams's bibliography, it seems that what counted as philosophy at UCLA is taken for theology at Yale!"

XII. EVILS AMONG THE PHILOSOPHERS

In my tradition, we have just devoted forty days, and especially yesterday, Good Friday, to facing the worst that human beings can suffer, be, and do—not just individual weakness and perversity but systemic evils, the ways that human societies and institutions privilege some while degrading others. Today, Holy Saturday, is a day of waiting and reflection. Accordingly, I want to draw this lecture to a close by noting some evils that plague professional philosophy as I have known it—to use the terminology of my tradition, some sins of which we should repent. I have already spoken about dogmatism, but I want to mention three more.

Professional philosophy as I have known it has been distorted by its
zeal for competitive advantage. It is a virtue to love excellence, but this
should dispose us to celebrate philosophical virtuosity wherever it is to
be found, to be awed and grateful in the presence of a David Lewis or
John Rawls that philosophical work can be done so well. Love of excellence should also inspire each of us to do and to want others to do as
well as we can. The determination to be better than others, to push
others down so that we may rise on the Leiter rankings, is very different. It clouds our philosophical judgment by giving us an incentive to
pour scorn on other people's work, and it poisons our profession with
contempt.

Perhaps next of kin is destructive criticism. There is a fine line between the use and abuse of analytic methods, with their demand for
clarity and precision, with their alertness to fallacious and confused
reasoning. Love of truth demands that we try to get it right. But we all
know the difference between exposing the weakness in someone else's
argument the better to leave them dangling and pointing out the problem but going on to brainstorm whether their thesis could not be defended, their idea developed in a better way. Pedagogy that disables is
abusive. In my time, I have watched too many (one would be too many)
philosophically talented, perhaps even potentially brilliant, philosophers get torn down by relentless dead-end critiques. Whenever and
wherever it happens, it is horrendous and puts our profession to shame.

Sexism is a sin of a different sort. We are all socialized to it, and—
like racism—it has to be peeled back one millimeter at a time. Certainly, it was worse in the sixties. When I applied to graduate school, my
advisor closed his recommendation with the reassuring sentence, "Miss
McCord shows no signs of getting married." When I got to Cornell, the
all-male faculty confessed at the newcomers party that they were worried about our class because they had admitted four women. When I
asked for the source of their concern, one said, "Well, if they're married
that's the problem, and if they're not married, that's the problem."
Another professor wondered, "What would happen if they got pregnant
and had a baby during the prelims?" I suggested that rescheduling
might be a plan. The four of us debated whether to sign our articles
with initials only, so that the gender discount would not be applied. In
fact, none of us ever did this. One of us went on to become a college
president. Two are senior members of the profession. Eventually, I

even had a secondary appointment in the (by them hallowed) philosophy faculty at Oxford. Our professors needn't have worried.

When Bob got a job at the University of Michigan, the nepotism rule was used to explain why I had to be a visiting lecturer. Three years later, when HEW threatened to cancel government grants unless the university improved its policy on women, Dick Brandt got me hired as a half-time assistant professor with a twelve-year tenure track. At UCLA, I was irritated to find myself among the token women on university-wide committees. But I saw that there was still a need for it even in the early nineties, when a former dean of a professional school argued for the promotion of his successor: "I was the first to admit women, but under her, we have more women than we know what to do with!" Oddly, theology is both more sexist and more politically correct. When I eventually went to Oxford as the first woman Regius Professor of Divinity, the hazing I got had much more to do with national origin than gender!

Through most of my career, I needed to believe that professional philosophy was meritarian. For me, it turned out to be not fair but fair enough. When white males persistently seized the victim role to whine about affirmative action, I eventually took to replying, "Well, we have to work three times as hard to get 75 percent credit. But it certainly makes for good work!" This is somewhat, but only somewhat, of an exaggeration.

NOTES

John Dewey Lecture delivered before the 85th annual Pacific Division Meeting of the American Philosophical Association in San Diego, California, on April 23, 2011. Used by permission of the John Dewey Foundation.

1. D. Z. Phillips, *The Concept of Prayer* (New York: Schocken Books, 1966).
2. J. L. Mackie, "Evil and Omnipotence," *Mind*, n.s., 64, 254 (1955): 200–212.
3. See Nelson Pike, "Divine Omniscience and Voluntary Action," *Philosophical Review* (January 1965), 7–46. See also the fruit of his further reflections: *God and Timelessness* (New York: Schocken Books, 1970), 53–86.
4. Robert Merrihew Adams, *Finite and Infinite Goods* (Oxford: Oxford University Press, 1999).

5. Marilyn McCord Adams, *William Ockham*, 2 vols. (Notre Dame, IN: University of Notre Dame Press, 1987, 1989).

6. William Alston, *Perceiving God* (Ithaca, NY: Cornell University Press, 1993).

7. Alvin Plantinga, *Warrant and Proper Function* (Oxford: Oxford University Press, 1993); *Warrant and the Current Debate* (Oxford: Oxford University Press, 1993) ; *Warrant and Christian Belief* (Oxford: Oxford University Press, 2000).

8. Richard Swinburne, *The Concept of Miracle* (London: Macmillan; New York: St. Martin's, 1970).

9. Richard Swinburne, *The Coherence of Theism* (Oxford: Clarendon, 1977).

10. Richard Swinburne, *The Existence of God* (Oxford: Clarendon, 1979).

11. For helpful discussions of the honor code, see J. G. Peristiany, ed., *Honour and Shame: The Values of Mediterranean Society* (London: Weidenfeld and Nicolson, 1966).

12. For an orientation to purity and defilement schemes, see Mary Douglas, *Purity and Danger: An Analysis of Concepts of Pollution and Taboo* (London: Routledge and Kegan Paul, 1966).

13. Marilyn McCord Adams, *Horrendous Evils and the Goodness of God* (Ithaca, NY: Cornell University Press, 1999); *Christ and Horrors: The Coherence of Christology* (Cambridge: Cambridge University Press, 2006).

8

UNNATURAL LOTTERIES AND DIVERSITY IN PHILOSOPHY

Claudia Card

In 1958, I took my first philosophy course from William H. Hay, later a Central APA president. I wrote my first philosophy paper on Williams James's *Varieties of Religious Experience* for an honors English course. If that's the beginning, my career spans five decades, most of it at the University of Wisconsin. Developments in that half century that impacted my work and changed its directions include the civil rights movement, the war in Vietnam, the birth of women's studies, gender studies, ethnic studies, queer studies, feminist philosophy and philosophy of race, Holocaust studies, environmentalism, and gay liberation. There was visible progress with the integration, at many levels, of philosophers of color into historically white academies. Philosophers with disabilities emerged from their closets. More children of working-class families went to college. (Tuition hikes are putting a damper on that trend.) These developments impacted not just my career but the areas of specialization in philosophy, courses available to students, the composition of departmental faculties, liaisons between philosophy and other programs, journals, article topics, APA sessions, as well as APA satellites and standing committees. Opening the field to such diversity enlarged the data of everyday life from which philosophical reflection begins. It enabled me to integrate my life outside the academy with my work within.

Technological changes have transformed how we communicate and publish, resulting in greater accessibility of information, especially important to women and minorities. I was more dependent on teachers and grapevines than are today's students and junior faculty. Not being in the loop is a serious issue, which the Internet mitigates. *Jobs for Philosophers* helped greatly (*Jobs in Philosophy* when introduced in the sixties) but not in time for my job search. I asked colleagues for years how to join the APA. They kept forgetting to find me an address or application. In 1974, Ruth Marcus asked if I would be on the Central APA Program Committee. She got me an application. Google solves that kind of problem today.

The editing capacities of word processing are a miracle for compulsive revisers like me. I wrote my senior thesis and my PhD dissertation on a portable manual Sears typewriter, one sheet of bond and two onion skin carbon copies, redoing each page with three errors or more.

Classroom atmospheres have changed. We used to tell students to put away newspapers. Now they have to turn off cell-phone ringers, portable radios, and CD players. Many open laptops (who knows what they do there). Teaching environments include terrifying developments. My university is in the heart of town. Anyone can walk in off the street. After digesting an article on fourteen campus shootings since the turn of the century, I told students to leave their cell phones on "vibrate," memorize room numbers and building names for all their classes, locate all exits, sit in a different seat each time, and we practiced getting down on the floor under the seats, to be sure we could do it and do it fast. I created an emergency code phrase, "Flight 93: Let's roll!" Our classrooms have no emergency buttons, but university administration has hinted at a text-messaging system to alert the campus.

My first career choice was chemistry, an ambition no one encouraged. My uncle George, blinded after a car accident, majored in philosophy before his law degree, and my father read him his assignments. I grew up hearing stories of their favorite philosophy professor, the pragmatist Max Otto. When I fell in love with philosophy, too, my father groaned, "Hardly a bread and butter subject!" A traveling salesman who lived on commission, he hoped I would qualify myself for a job with more security than he had or, failing that, have the good sense to marry someone who did. He lived just long enough to see me tenured at Wisconsin and to realize that I would never marry anyone.

I had chosen a philosophy major but had no idea where I could go with it. My advisor, Marcus Singer, also later a Central APA president, had just published a book, *Generalization in Ethics*, that earned him instant international fame. On his advice, and with support from my teachers Robert Ammerman and Gerald MacCallum, I applied to graduate schools that I would otherwise never have had the nerve to consider. Hearing of my ambitions, a Wisconsin philosophy graduate student undertook to inform me that no university would hire a woman to teach philosophy. My teacher Julius Weinberg then spent an afternoon telling me his life story, to give me hope. One of his teachers had argued at a faculty meeting that it would be a waste to offer a fellowship to a Jewish student because "Who would hire a Jew?" My teachers were the generation that crashed anti-Semitic barriers in American academies. Bernie Gert told me two decades later when I was a "Visiting Associate Witch" at Dartmouth that he was in the first wave of Jewish professors hired on that campus at the end of the 1950s. These philosophers set the stage for my generation to crash the gender barriers and the race barriers and to open the closets of lesbian and gay philosophers and of philosophers with disabilities.

Not all my teachers were as sensitive as these. One who taught French existentialism (not the one who teaches it now) regularly spiced his lectures with such jokes as that it is impossible to rape a woman because she can run faster with her skirt up than a man with his pants down. I laughed along with the rest but with mixed feelings that I did not yet understand.

In eight years as a university student, I had two female teachers, neither a philosopher. But an impressive five of seventeen in my entering graduate class at Harvard were female. By second semester, two remained: Sharon Bishop and me. Francis Dauer, a couple years ahead of me, was a teaching fellow for Quine's logic; everyone else looked Caucasian. Nevertheless, and despite a brutal system of preliminary examinations, the early sixties was an exciting time to be at Harvard. My first year there, 1962, was Jack Rawls's first year there, too. Stanley Cavell arrived the next year and taught a unique philosophy of religion course on ten atheists. Robert Nozick came as I was writing my dissertation (I audited his classes for fun). All three eventually became Eastern APA presidents. My Harvard graduate-student contemporaries included David Lewis, David Lyons, Thomas E. Hill Jr., Thomas Nagel, Tim Scanlon, Allan Gibbard, Alan Fuchs, Michael Slote, Michael Stocker, Paul Eisenberg, Paul Gomberg, Onora O'Neill, Ted Cohen from

Hume, Illinois, and Steve Smith from What Cheer, Iowa. I was from Pardeeville, Wisconsin. We suspected Harvard of practicing a little geographical affirmative action.

I chose Harvard to study with Rawls. "Two Concepts of Rules" and "Justice as Fairness" knocked my sox off when I was writing my senior thesis. I applied also to Princeton, assuming that if Harvard took women, everyone must. Princeton rejected me for being female. I received a letter from a place I had never heard of called "Radcliffe" and was about to toss it when I wondered aloud to a friend why this place I had never even applied to was accepting me into its graduate program. That is how I learned I was going to Harvard (for me, Harvard-Radcliffe, the first year).

Again, I was fortunate in my teachers. Besides Rawls and Cavell, there were Roderick Firth, Morton White, and visitors William Frankena, Julius Moravcsik, and Willis Doney. I was a teaching fellow for Henry Aiken, who set an entertaining example of lecturing to the masses, teaching them Moses to Marx in one semester, to alternate clapping and hissing.

Feminism had not yet come to Harvard. Lamont Library was men only, women barred at the front door. Yet men could enter Radcliffe Library and check out books. Despite dress codes for undergraduates to prevent women being mistaken for men, most women were invisible to most instructors. At Wisconsin, I was an enthusiastically vocal undergraduate. At Harvard, I shut up and listened for four years, a habit that persisted for a decade. We were being leafleted by Black Panthers on Boston Common, waiting to see the film *Tom Jones*, when my friend Charles Parsons asked me if I was a feminist. I said, "What's a feminist?" It was 1963.

Jack Rawls proved as amazing as his essays and as courageous as he was generous. At a time when "go for the jugular" was the prevailing mode of philosophical repartee, Rawls disarmed critics by saying, "Well you are probably right. However . . ." Always kind, he set a powerful counterexample. It is there in his writings, too. When he cites work of others who are living (often even of those no longer living), it is usually to build on something positive in their work or explain how it would be a natural view to hold, even if he ultimately disagrees.

Those who never heard Rawls lecture may not realize how formidable his stutter could be. This was an era when prospective employers routinely asked recommenders whether the candidate had any physical disabilities or problems that might interfere with effectiveness in teaching (you see where the burden of effectiveness lay). Interviewers at that time also asked female candidates (married or not) if we used birth control (even what methods) and whether we planned to have children. This is what that graduate student who warned me meant: no one would hire someone who would soon leave to raise children (you see the assumptions about who would raise them). My advisor had dutifully warned me my senior year that I would have to be twice as good as my male competitors, as he had to be in the early fifties in relation to non-Jewish rivals. Imagine how good Rawls must have thought he had to be with that stutter to make his living by giving lectures. After a bit, the stutter calmed down, we tuned in, and years later, some noticed a semi-stuttering pattern in the way we spoke when deep in philosophical thought.

Rawls's lectures on social and political philosophy were handwritten, word for word, on yellow legal pads, drafts of chapters for *A Theory of Justice*. He let us type these lectures onto ditto masters, reproduce them, and circulate them among ourselves (I did several on that portable manual Sears typewriter). Later, he made student copies available at cost in the Harvard Coop book annex. Each week so many lined up at his office that only a fraction got to see him. Yet he made time for lunch with me one day my first semester. His final exam, preceded by a review sheet, included one mandatory question, which he told us in advance: develop an objection to the lecturer's theory of justice. His teaching fellows told us later he never graded anyone down for their answer to that question.

Some philosophers of the generation of my teachers who had a great influence on me were people I never knew personally. Three among my early models were H. L. A. Hart, Joel Feinberg, and Herbert Morris. They had significant impacts on my career; in Hart's case, more than I realized until recently. A couple years ago, I read Nicola Lacey's marvelous biography of Hart, full of revelations that put his work into a context he could never quite make explicit. Hart's book *The Concept of Law* was a text in Frankena's ethics seminar (as was Singer's *Generalization in Ethics*) and in Rawls's political philosophy course my first semester of graduate school. Hart's essays on punishment were foundational for my undergraduate thesis and PhD dissertation on that topic.

His feisty little book *Law, Liberty, Morality* argued against Lord Devlin on homosexuality. His classic essay "Are There Any Natural Rights?" appeared in the same volume of the *Philosophical Review* as "Two Concepts of Rules" and is the acknowledged source of Rawls's duty of fair play. Such essays fueled my ambitions to become a philosopher. Yet I was astonished on reading Lacey's biography to learn, through quotations from Hart's letters and diaries, that he identified from an early age as a "repressed homosexual." No one in the philosophical world knew this. Nor did many know his grandparents were Jewish immigrants to England. Hart was neither religious nor a political activist. Although aware of his general sexual orientation, he developed what he found when it was new to be a good sexual relationship with the woman he married in 1941, to whom he stayed married and with whom he had four children. But Lacey reports that Hart lost interest in sex after the first child and never ceased ruminating on his sexuality. She traces the influence of his repression on his passionate advocacy of reforms in the law regarding consensual sex between adults. Learning this gave me a new appreciation of Hart's work and its contribution to mine. It would have been so validating to me as an undergraduate, deeply closeted in many of the same ways, to know that this intellectual giant whose work I so admired had passions like my own. Yet he had no more context than I had then for making such facts public without exposing himself to being diagnosed as mentally ill. His work laid groundwork for my generation to go a bit further, to create, for example, an APA Committee on the Status of LGBT People in the Profession.

Another such influence was Simone de Beauvoir, whose work I began to read in that undergraduate existentialism course. She never came out publicly as lesbian, although it was general knowledge that she lived with a female companion for many years, to the end of her life. She lost an early teaching job over her association with a female student. But she went on to write a chapter in *The Second Sex* that philosophically defended lesbianism as a choice. I did a paper on that chapter in the existentialism course and later wrote an essay on it that eventually appeared in *Hypatia* and then developed into a chapter in my first book, *Lesbian Choices*.

Wisconsin hired me in 1966, one chapter done on my dissertation, another in progress. I taught three courses each semester (three preps, two large lectures). There were no sabbaticals. The late sixties and early seventies were deeply troubled times for our campus, as for many others. My second year of teaching, violence broke out with the demonstration of October 18, 1967, protesting the campus presence of Dow Chemical—maker of napalm—to interview graduating seniors. (Had I become a chemist, would I have viewed that event differently?) The next semester, in May 1968, eighteen-year-old Christine Rothschild in my honors introductory course was found murdered on campus, attacked apparently on her early morning walk. The case has never been solved, nor is the motive known. In May of this year [2008], I will speak at a memorial service on campus on the fortieth anniversary of her death. The years 1967–1971 saw multiple demonstrations, teargas, and trashing for many causes, including protest of the shootings of Kent State students in May 1970, demands for a black studies program, and demands for a teaching assistants' association. In spring 1970, I held classes in my living room to avoid the teargas on campus. My introductory honors class that semester included seventeen-year-old David Fine. That summer he became one of the Sterling Hall four (two others were philosophy graduate students) wanted by the FBI in the bombing of the Army-Math Research Center. Unknown to them at the time, physicist Robert Fassnacht was at work in the basement in the wee hours. He died in their explosion.

By then, I was teaching a popular course called "Crime and Punishment," populated with students who had first-hand acquaintance with criminal justice. Some had been jailed for demonstrating illegally or possessing grass. One was assigned to guard the brig in the Marine Corps. Others had grave encounters. One was found not guilty by reason of insanity of the murder of an abusive spouse. Another did time in prison and a mental institution for sexual abuse of children. He seemed little more than a child himself. A woman in her thirties, recently released from an institution thanks to the efforts of a staff worker, had been confined there by her father at age thirteen for being out of his control. (I did not know then that such confinement could mean she had refused his sexual advances or threatened to expose him or tried to run away from him.) Students voluntarily presented these histories in papers they read to the class. It struck me that I was just lucky their experiences were not mine. I began to wonder whether my approach to punishment was coming from a perspective that was not true to the experience of people like me—people of my social class, my gender, my sexual orientation. I was trained to locate myself philosophically in relation to positions in books, the world of the library. My students located themselves philosophically in relation to their experiences with real crime and punishment. I would later take that approach also, not to crime and punishment but to feminism and sexual politics as a female who refused social norms for good women.

The year I was up for tenure (fall 1971) was the year I connected with feminism. María Lugones, then a Wisconsin graduate student, organized a consciousness-raising (CR) group. For three years, I attended its weekly meetings with enthusiasm. Those discussions started to transform my thinking about philosophy and my position in the profession. Had I connected with feminism one year earlier, I would almost certainly not have been tenurable at Wisconsin. But I would not have known that. After I was promoted, I saw how feminist work was evaluated in a tenure decision and a retention decision. Had that CR group formed earlier, the slenderness of my CV would have been blamed on my feminism, and the prognosis for my productivity would have been grim, as there was then no recognized body of feminist philosophy. As it was, the slenderness of my CV was blamed on the two-and-a-half years it took me to complete my dissertation, and the prognosis for my productivity was optimistic, given the testimonials of Hart, Feinberg, and Morris, who knew me only through my published work. Twenty-two years elapsed before my department tenured a second woman, ten more before the third. The trajectory is right, although the third woman left at once.

A woman has not yet chaired my department. I consented to stand for election more than a decade ago, assuming others would just be glad to be off the hook (the spirit in which my department had previously elected by accolade anyone who seemed willing). That election was a fiasco but also a fortuitous turning point in my career. A younger colleague with an interest in being chair graciously declined to run against me, though he would surely have been elected (he has been since). Another colleague (now retired) nominated everyone he could think of to run against me. All but one declined. The chair announced a tie vote and then told me the other candidate would withdraw if I would, because it would be bad to have a chair elected by a slim margin. Odd, I thought. My rival could increase the margin by withdrawing even if I didn't. I refused, figuring a woman could only be elected by a slim margin, and she could then demonstrate the same competence as her male peers. I circulated a list of my administrative experience; my rival did not, and the chair declined to require it. The process was repeated, from nomination to vote, with identical results. By then, I was physically ill from stress, an indication that administration was probably not my forte. We both withdrew, and a previous chair agreed to serve. But luck was with me. With time and energy available to write that would otherwise have gone into serving the department, and with freedom to apply for grants, I wrote more books and consequently received more speaking invitations and more grant support than I had dreamed of. Surprised everybody, not least myself. But that is getting ahead of the story.

In the early seventies, more radical transformations of my teaching and writing were yet to come. In fall 1976, I connected with the Midwest Society of Women in Philosophy. SWIP was founded in 1971 when Sandra Bartky and others responded to a call for a feminist caucus at the Central APA. SWIP became the largest influence on my subsequent development. In twenty years, I missed only two of its semiannual meetings on different campuses. In 1976, I met Joyce Trebilcot, Marilyn Frye, Sandra Bartky, Iris Young, Margaret Simons, and, at the next one, Alison Jaggar. Nineteen seventy-six saw Carol Gould's and Marx Wartofsky's anthology *Women and Philosophy*, with such wonderful essays as Christine Pierce's "Holes and Slime in Sartre's Psychoanalysis." Next year brought Jane English's *Sex Equality* (she died a year later climbing the Matterhorn) and her coedited *Feminism and Philosophy*, with Mary Vetterling-Braggin and Frederick Elliston, which had four papers on rape—first time I saw rape taken up in a philosophy paper where the issue was not protecting men from false accusations. Marilyn Frye, coauthor of one of those papers, became my model of wielding techniques of analytic philosophy with a feminist pen.

To my unanticipated delight, at SWIP, I felt neither defensive nor invisible. I knew scarcely anything of feminist philosophy and so did not anticipate a warm welcome as I read my contribution to a panel on the question "Are Virtues Sex-Related?" But SWIP then was committed to supporting every woman curious enough to come. Rousing discussions elicited the best potentialities of each paper. SWIP heard me back into speech and became the audience for whom I wrote. There was then no feminist philosophy journal (*Hypatia* came later, a brainchild of SWIP). I thought no philosophy journal would ever be interested in publishing what I was writing. I did it because I could. I had tenure. I believed in it. Students then were keenly interested in it. But most of all, I enjoyed it! I had not had that much fun doing philosophy since I was an undergraduate.

Stanley Cavell used to speak of a rapport that enables people to finish each other's sentences. We could be like that at SWIP but not because we held the same views. Our approaches were Marxist, socialist, radicalesbian, and liberal, differences we took seriously. But good will ran deep, as did commonalities in experiences not shared by our male colleagues.

With behind-the-scenes support from my late colleague John Moulton, assistant to many chairs of my department, I taught a course called "Feminism and Sexual Politics" every semester for years. It was the first feminist philosophy course at Dartmouth when I visited in 1978–79. I did it again at the University of Pittsburgh in 1980. In 1981, I created a historical companion course, "Classics in Feminist Theory," a title that was fun when feminist philosophy was not part of the standard curriculum. That course featured Mary Wollstonecraft, Margaret Fuller, Sojourner Truth, Ida Wells, Friedrich Engels, John Stuart Mill, Charlotte Perkins Gilman, Emma Goldman, and Virginia Woolf, sandwiched between the French Revolution and World War II.

In May 1978, I presented my "coming out" paper, "Feminist Ethical Theory: A Lesbian Perspective," at Minnesota to an overflow crowd in the law school auditorium. Kathy Addelson (then Kathy Parsons) had been invited to present a paper to which I had replied at a conference in Madison. Although we had met just that once, she insisted to Minnesota that I be invited to respond again. So each of us was invited to give a main paper, with the other commenting. We occupied the stage jointly both times, as a matter of feminist and anarchist principle, rejecting hierarchies and heroes. That level of support gave me new courage. I have written of that occasion as the day on which I literally found my voice. Since graduate school, when I shut up and listened, my voice had become soft; I routinely asked those in the back of the room to wave a paper if they could not hear me. There in Minneapolis, I was as surprised as anyone by the voice that came booming out. No microphone. Was I angry? Not with that audience. They were as respectful as I have seen. I expected some might ask what was philosophical about all that.

No one did. They asked great questions. I began that day to make up for years of silence and to listen with a different ear.

That fall, I went to Dartmouth College on a year's visiting appointment. Dartmouth knew me from the work that got me tenured. Willis Doney may have remembered me from his visiting appointment at Harvard, when I took his rationalist course. But Dartmouth had not yet seen my radicalesbian feminist incarnation. I had heard that Dartmouth tended to be conservative and so wondered if a year there would be a good experience for me. After discussing it with my therapist, I proposed that they invite me first to give a lecture, so we could look each other over. They did. All bets were off. We had a great time, and my year there was very positive. It was the first year of Dartmouth's Women's Studies Program (I was a guest member) and Hanover, New Hampshire's first Take Back the Night march. Students demonstrated to abolish admissions quotas for women, wearing T-shirts emblazoned with the letters "BTMFD"—"Burn the Motherfuckers Down" or "Benevolent Teachers and Mothers for Democracy," depending who asked. A highlight for me was the interdisciplinary Faculty Seminar for Feminist Inquiry. It met monthly over dinner funded by the college to discuss a member's paper we all read in advance. That was the most intellectually exciting faculty group I had experienced without feeling like an outsider (remarkable, considering that I was in fact a visitor).

That fall, Mary Daly's *Gyn/Ecology: The Meta-Ethics of Radical Feminism* and Susan Griffin's *Woman and Nature: The Roaring Inside Her* were published, with radical feminist takes on the European witch burnings. I ordered both for my spring course and began signing my letters "Visiting Associate Witch" (to the distress of colleagues at both Dartmouth and Wisconsin; maybe one reason Wisconsin promoted me after twelve years was to get rid of that "associate"). I taught Adrienne Rich's *Of Woman Born* and Kate Millett's *Sexual Politics*. There was nothing in treatise form by radical feminists with the kind of philosophical training I had, and the door was revolving quick for non-tenured feminists who did. I mimeographed SWIP papers and assigned Marilyn Frye's essay on separatism, which circulated as a pamphlet before morphing into a chapter in *The Politics of Reality*. Each day that Dartmouth classroom held more women, on the floors and window sills and in each other's laps. They were literally coming in off the streets of Hanover. It was an exciting time to be creating feminist philosophy.

SWIP and Mary Daly led me deeper into Continental philosophy. Infamous for her tenure battle at Boston College, Daly was the first feminist philosopher to write a treatise perfect for my course. *Gyn/ Ecology* was funny, radical, in-your-face, openly lesbian, ambitious, feisty, visionary, and philosophical to the core. Daly refused to take questions from men in discussions following her invited lectures (she would interact with them at receptions afterward). The Dartmouth religion department met to consider whether to disinvite her when they learned that. An outraged member of the department is reported to have exclaimed, "I have never discriminated against anyone on the basis of his sex!"

With funds from Dartmouth, I attended the first full day of feminist philosophy of science at the AAAS Convention in Houston and participated in the first National Women's Studies Association convention in Lawrence, Kansas. At NWSA, I met Azizah al-Hibri, soon to be *Hypatia*'s first editor. Later, she invited me to speak at the 1984 Beauvoir conference in Philadelphia, which Beauvoir initially planned to attend. That invitation set off a chain of events that culminated in my editing *The Cambridge Companion to Simone de Beauvoir*. Who would have thought a year at Dartmouth in 1978–79 could be so stimulating and influential for a novice radicalesbian philosopher? Returning to Wisconsin, I joined its Women's Studies Program.

Almost twenty years after I was hired, I read a paper to my department, which until then had operated heavily in go-for-the-jugular. They were so decent to me that I then did it often, occasionally to crowds, mandating change to a large auditorium. Almost twenty years after I was hired, a graduate student received the PhD under my direction (twelve have done so since; seven more are on their way). Nearly twenty years elapsed before I presented an APA symposium paper. As I see it now, in my first decade of teaching, I was still in the shut up and listen mode. The next decade was an apprenticeship in feminism, in which I was searching for my voice, working to undo four decades of patriarchal socialization. By the nineties, I was ready to speak in my own voice. All my books, with the exception of one coedited textbook anthology, have been published since I turned fifty.

It is impossible to overestimate the importance of networking by SWIP and other feminist philosophy organizations, such as the Society for Analytical Feminism, for crashing gender barriers in philosophy. My first feminist appearances on Central APA main programs were through SWIP connections: Alison Jaggar on the Central APA Program Committee in 1981 suggested me as a respondent to Richard Brandt. I did a lot of homework for the session, reading not only his very long paper but also his most recent book. He appreciated that and wrote a reply to my reply (handing it to me the night before at the hotel). I then replied to his reply to my reply (handing it to him at our session), and, thanks to Kai Nielsen in the audience, the whole thing appeared in the *Canadian Journal of Philosophy*. Suddenly, I had proof that my work could get published in a philosophy journal even though everything I now wrote was permeated by feminism. Then Marilyn Frye on the Central APA Program Committee in 1984 proposed me for an invited paper, for which I wrote "Gender and Moral Luck," the essay that started me writing *The Unnatural Lottery*. My working title for *The Unnatural Lottery* had been *Character and Moral Luck*, which my publisher thought was not a very saleable title, and so, in a moment of inspiration, I proposed *The Unnatural Lottery*, playing on Rawls's natural lottery. Rawls's natural lottery referred to one's luck in the natural advantages or disadvantages with which one is born; he liked the idea that justice might somewhat compensate those unlucky in the natural lottery. My *un*natural lottery referred to advantageous and disadvantageous starting points in life that are defined by unjust social institutions, positions Rawls's principles would rule out.

Feminist separatism was a defining theme in my work for most of two decades. It was critical to disrupting habits of seeing myself through patriarchal eyes. It took such forms as reading almost exclusively materials by rebellious women (which I did for several years; even so, I never caught up) and writing to audiences of women. Yet I also wanted to justify those who had stuck their necks out to support me through undergraduate and graduate school and the tenure and promotional processes, all of them men. I wanted to give something back that they also could value, to give them reason not to regret having supported me. Bernard Williams's and Thomas Nagel's exchange that introduced the concept of moral luck resonated with so much in my experience that I wanted to build something on that concept. You can see from what I have already told you how much luck has been a factor in what I have been able to do. And so, in 1986, after that invited APA paper and with my first sabbatical leave (one semester, after twenty years), I began writing *The Unnatural Lottery*, thinking to myself, "If I write a chapter a year, in ten years, I will have a book." In ten years, I had two books, two edited volumes, and a guest-edited issue of *Hypatia*. I was on a roll. I had become what my colleagues used to call "a late bloomer," although the blossoms were not what they had once anticipated.

Besides SWIP, three sources of inspiration and irritation fueled my writing from 1985 to 1995. The first was a course on lesbian culture that I taught in Women's Studies (a far more stressful experience than the election fiasco of 1997). The second was the new journal *Hypatia*, which published several of my SWIP papers. Third was a philosophical correspondence with philosopher Richard Mohr of the University of Illinois. Mohr became my most generous and reliable critic. By "generous," I don't mean his comments were nice. They reflected careful reading. They were specific and constructive. They were amazingly prompt. And they helped me a lot. Author of *Gays/Justice* published by Columbia University Press in 1988, Mohr was the first editor of Columbia's new book series Between Men / Between Women. He mobilized me to submit a proposal for the book that became *Lesbian Choices*, which is how I came to be writing two books at once. Cheshire Calhoun noted on the APA "author meets critics" panel that *Lesbian Choices* seems to have two audiences: in the early chapters, a lesbian feminist audience, but in the last section, a mixed-gender gay audience. Truth is, early chapters address Midwest SWIP and students in the lesbian culture course; the last chapters address Richard Mohr.

The journal *Hypatia* was born in the early 1980s as three special issues of the Women's Studies International Quarterly/Forum. That umbilical cord was severed when Indiana University Press agreed to publish *Hypatia* as an independent journal. Margaret Simons was its first editor after the emancipation. An early issue included my essay on Beauvoir's lesbian chapter in *The Second Sex*.

Lesbian Choices was a transitional work. It began as an alternative to the care ethic of Sarah Hoagland's 1988 book *Lesbian Ethics*. For Hoagland, justice was not an important value. For me, justice remained vital, even if not the centerpiece of ethics I had once thought it. Hoagland's *Lesbian Ethics* was an alternative to the care ethics of Sara Ruddick's book *Mothering* and Nel Noddings's book *Caring*. Ruddick and Noddings took as paradigms of caring idealized adult-child relationships. Hoagland's paradigms of caring were relationships between equals. I departed from all three. Retaining a sense of the critical importance of justice from people who are neither friends nor acquaintances, even people one may never know, led me into social issues on which Mohr often had a very different take from my own (pornography, for example, and more recently, marriage). By including gay men in my audience, I was learning to insert my philosophical ideas into conversations among philosophers of both genders who could not complete my sentences the way SWIP members sometimes could. I had once known perfectly well how to do that or I would never have survived graduate school and probationary employment. But I found I had to learn again after rebirth as a radical feminist. Transition to a wider audience was facilitated also by environmental ethics, a longstanding feminist cause. Susan Griffin's *Woman and Nature*, which fired my interest in 1978, was an important text a decade later in my large, cross-listed environmental-ethics lecture course.

In 1988, the late John Pugh of John Carroll University met with Sarah Hoagland and me at Central APA in Cincinnati to form the Society for Lesbian and Gay Philosophy (SLGP, pronounced "slag-pee"). Pugh and I were the first cochairs. Sandra Bartky, on the APA Board, encouraged us to become an APA satellite so we could hold sessions at conventions. The rule was that to apply for such status, an organization had to list its members. Yet, to induce philosophers to join our organization, we had assured them of privacy. The compromise we negotiated was that we would provide a sample list of those who consented to have their names published. Our list included supportive members whose own orientation was neither lesbian nor gay. This organization had been John Pugh's dream for years. He died a few years later and left the society a bequest. Richard Mohr and Mark Chekola were also important engines behind the scenes. Mohr, Ed Stein, and Judith Butler were on SLGP's first APA session held in Atlanta in 1989, exchanging views on the social construction of sexuality. Less than a decade later, in 1997, I chaired the new APA Committee on the Status of Lesbian, Gay, Bisexual, and Transgender People in the Profession. Philosophy has come a long way on sexuality since days when Professor Henry Aiken could wake up a lecture hall full of Harvard undergraduates with jokes about the economic system of the "lazy fairies."

During the 1980s, Midwest SWIP also evolved. María Lugones, then at Carleton College in Northfield, Minnesota, introduced a women of color caucus, which became a regular part of every conference. The ethos of Midwest SWIP came to include the expectation of sensitivity to race and class in every paper. Before SWIP, the only African American woman philosophy professor I had heard of was Angela Davis. The only African American male philosopher I had met was Laurence Thomas. At SWIP, I met Jackie Anderson who taught at Olive-Harvey College in Chicago. At other conferences in the 1980s and early '90s, I met and studied the works also of Bernard Boxill, Howard McGary, Bill Lawson, Lou Outlaw, Leonard Harris, Charles Mills, Michele Moody-Adams, Tommy Lott, La Verne Shelton, Naomi Zack, and more. At the turn of the century, I escorted through graduation the first African American woman to receive the PhD from my department.

Works by contemporary philosophers of color made me curious about the work of earlier generations of philosophers of color. I began inserting their texts into my courses in ethics and American philosophy. Philosophers on the coasts probably did this earlier than I did. Certainly, Leonard Harris did at Purdue. In Madison, Wisconsin, it was unusual for students of color to turn up in philosophy classes. That began to change as I put the texts of philosophers of color onto the syllabus. In introductory ethics, at the end of a unit on egoism, we read W. E. B. Du Bois on his experience of "twoness"—having two selves. In chapter 1 of *The Souls of Black Folk*, he writes of tensions between what he calls his "Negro self" and what he calls his "American self." He poses the ethical challenge of how to resolve those tensions without abandoning either self. Egoism is no help when the question is which ego or what kind of ego to develop. Later, when my ethics course takes up Immanuel Kant on duties to oneself, we read Boxill and Thomas on protesting injustice to oneself and on the dispute between Du Bois and Booker T. Washington over the most self-respecting ways to respond to racism in America.

By the mid-nineties, I had ceased teaching courses devoted to feminism, working much of that material into everything else I taught. Now there were many feminist philosophy groups and conferences. Iris Young held a conference at the University of Pittsburgh on feminist social and political philosophy. Thanks to Linda Lopez McAlister's work as a U.S. liaison to the International Association of Women Philosophers (IAPh), I connected with that group with consequences for all the work I have done since 1995. Its usually biennial meetings are in a different country each time. Most have been in Europe; once in Boston;

in summer 2008, Korea. Again, I reoriented, this time toward an international audience not totally feminist, although receptive. I began to write about genocide, war rape, terrorism, and torture, topics of my current work. That international orientation led to invitations to speak in Beijing and Brazil. Again, networks of women were key in structuring my research, teaching, and outreach opportunities.

My current work on torture, terrorism, and genocide addresses the problem of how to respond to atrocities without perpetrating atrocities oneself in responding. The challenge is to find ways to respond that preserve humanitarian values. Torture, for example, is one current response to terrorism, insofar as it is used to extract information regarding suspected terrorists. But torture fails the test of preserving humanitarian values. Much of this work is not focused on women. Yet all of it is permeated and shaped by my experience with feminism.

"Feminist" does not figure in the name of IAPh. Most feminist work in its symposia is from the Americas. A decade ago, feminist philosophy was not a recognized subject in northern European universities. To fill that gap in their curricula, feminist students at the Goethe University in Frankfurt organized to bring over feminist philosophers from the U.S. Nancy Fraser, Wendy Brown, and Iris Young were among those brought over. In 1999, they invited me to teach a block seminar on "Feminist Ethics in the U.S." There I enjoyed meeting Angelika Krebs and Axel Honneth. I read my "Gray Zones" paper to the Frankfurt philosophy department and again in Freiburg the next weekend. "Gray zones" is a concept I stole from Primo Levi's book *The Drowned and the Saved*. In gray zones, people who are already targets of evil become complicit in inflicting on others the very evils they face themselves. Levi's main example was death squads with crematorium duty at Auschwitz. I explored the cases of mothers binding their daughters' feet and children incinerating their parents for violating sexist norms. It was quite an experience discussing that paper with a German audience, especially in Freiburg where Heidegger had taught. But it was not the Freiburg philosophy department. The economics department invited me, a result of a lovely hour spent with two of their graduate students, Doro Schmidt and Nils Goldschmidt, in my office when they visited Wisconsin a year or two before.

The year I went to Germany, I was writing *The Atrocity Paradigm*. Before he left for Harvard, Dan Wikler and I applied to Wisconsin's

Center for Jewish Studies for a development grant to create a course on ethical issues pertaining to the Holocaust. When he left, I developed and taught the course myself and accepted an invitation to join the Center for Jewish Studies.

FEAST—the Society for Feminist Ethics and Social Philosophy— was born in the aftermath of the "Feminist Ethics Revisited" conference of 1999 in Tampa. Joan Callahan was its midwife and namer. Shortly thereafter, FEMSS, Feminist Epistemology, Metaphysics, and Science Studies, was created. Thanks to initiatives by Anita Superson and Samantha Brennan, the Society for Analytical Feminism held an independent conference in London, Ontario, in 2004 and another in Kentucky this spring, after years of APA satellite meetings. The Society for the Study of Women Philosophers has held APA satellite sessions for decades, and there is now a Society for Interdisciplinary Feminist Phenomenology with contact Bonnie Mann at the University of Oregon. (Her philosophy department requires every PhD student to take two courses or seminars in feminist philosophy.) There is talk in some of these organizations of creating more than one new feminist philosophy journal, and some formal steps are underway.

If I would not have been tenurable at the University of Wisconsin had I discovered feminism a year earlier, for the past decade the philosophy department and the university have warmly and materially supported my work. A well-published female colleague is coming up for tenure in much less than ten years since the last one. I no longer leave department meetings with my stomach tied in knots. (True, we are not exactly the same department, which makes it easier to recount some of this history.)

Yet the past also lingers and has consequences. My department no longer awards its sexist fellowship because that fellowship is awardable only to men by apparently unbreakable terms of the will of its donor. But past recipients are encouraged to gift the department when they can to support research by graduate women. A past recipient, currently chair of an Ivy League philosophy department, recently did just that.

Activities that used to count against me have become the occasion for awards. In 2001, when Dan Hausman was chair, he recommended me (to my complete surprise) for a Wisconsin Alumni Research Professorship (that's WARF, the folks who brought us the rat poison Warfarin). Recipients name their WARF professorships, which is how I became the Emma Goldman Professor of Philosophy. Marilyn Frye, Alison Jaggar, and Margaret Simons have received comparably prestigious awards at their institutions, and others of our peers whom I cannot yet mention have been nominated. Imagine the awards Iris Young would continue to receive, were she here with us.

With support from Noël Carroll and Hausman again, I received in 2002 a five-year senior fellowship at the Institute for Research in the Humanities, which cut my course load in half for the duration. That appointment gave me regular access to the most stimulating interdisciplinary faculty groups I had experienced since the Dartmouth faculty seminar for feminist inquiry. In 2004, when Larry Shapiro was chair and Shelley Glodowski administrator, I was allowed to inherit a retired colleague's corner office. Walls of windows look out on Lake Mendota to my left and the state capitol to my right. The other two walls are lined with six bookcases and six file cabinets enabling me for the first time in decades to put everything away. That is where I write, five days a week, early morning to late afternoon (when I am not on the road and my wrist is not broken from falling on ice in what we cheerfully call "the spring semester"). After nearly three decades in an office the size of a prison cell, I love my current work environment with its coven of thirteen witches hanging from the ceiling.

I mention these developments not just to boast (although they are surely worth boasting of) but to credit my department and university for their current support, to put these perks into a perspective that includes my teachers who helped make it possible for me to survive to enjoy them, and to encourage younger feminist philosophers and other radical philosophers to hang in there (no pun intended). My hope is that philosophers of my generation will have done for younger philosophers who are creatively striving to do philosophy in a new key as much as philosophers of my teachers' generation had done for us.

NOTE

John Dewey Lecture delivered before the 105th annual Central Division Meeting of the American Philosophical Association in Chicago, Illinois, on April 17, 2008. Used by permission of the John Dewey Foundation.

INDEX

Adams, Robert Merrihew (Bob), 79, 137, 142, 149
Addelson, Kathy, 160
Adler, Mortimer, 67
aesthetics, 6, 11, 14, 19–20. *See also* art
affirmative action, 149
African Americans: activism of, 78; and civil rights movement, 92; in philosophy, 27, 165–166
African American studies, 12, 36
AIDS, 146
Aiken, Henry David, 6, 7, 154, 165
Albritton, Rogers, 30, 31, 34, 134, 137
Allen, Woody, 87
Alston, Bill, 131, 142
Ambrose, Alice, 31
American Association of University Women, 73
American Philosophical Association (APA), 1–3, 34, 37, 39, 41, 44n7, 44n8, 77, 81, 83, 99, 141, 151, 165
Ammerman, Robert, 152
Analysis (journal), 91
analytic ethics, 31, 35
analytic philosophy: British idealism vs., 12; continental philosophy vs., 11, 90, 99–100, 117–118, 120; criticisms of, 21, 91, 118; and feminism, 159, 162; history of, 48, 49, 55; and history of philosophy, 15–16, 19, 33, 91, 122, 133, 140; and limits of thought, 13,

13–14; and medieval philosophy, 139, 140; and philosophy of religion, 130, 136
Anderson, Alan, 78
Anderson, Jackie, 165
Anglo-idealism, 68. *See also* British idealism
Anscombe, Elizabeth, 132
Anselm, 135, 136
anti-foundationalism, 21, 40
antirealism, 133, 133–134
anti-Semitism, 25, 26, 152
applied ethics, 35
Aquinas, Thomas, 135, 136, 137, 140, 141
Arendt, Hannah, 95, 97–98, 100, 101
Aristotle, 7, 9, 15, 54, 75, 100, 130, 131, 133, 140, 143
art, 22. *See also* aesthetics
artificial intelligence, 124
Asher, Nick, 81
Association of Symbolic Logic, 78
Austin, J. L., 13, 50, 66
Ayer, A. J., 35, 48

Baier, Kurt, 35
Baltimore Orioles (baseball team), 110
Barnard College, 47–48, 53, 54, 55
Bartky, Sandra, 77, 159, 165
Batkin, Norton, 116
Beardsley, Monroe, 11, 19, 70
Beauvoir, Simone de, 156, 162, 164

belief, 54, 59, 81
Believers, vs. Consequentialists, 58, 59–60
Belnap, Nuel, 78, 81
Benhabib, Seyla, 95
Berkeley, George, 7, 47, 51, 133, 140
Bernacerraf, Paul, 81
Bernays, Paul, 68
Bernstein, Carol, 87, 94, 98, 99, 100
Bernstein, Richard, 9
Bett, Richard, 39
Bible, 143, 144
Bishop, Sharon, 153
Black, Max, 27, 28, 29, 112, 132
black studies. *See* African American
   studies
Blanshard, Brand, 8
Bloom, Allan, 87
Bloom, Harold, 29
Boas, George, 109
Boethius, 136, 137
Bohr, Niels, 124
Bosanquet, Bernard, 68
Bouwsma, O. K., 7, 23
Boxill, Bernard, 165, 166
Bradley, F. H., 68
the brain, 123
Braithwaite, R. B., 51
Brandt, Richard (Dick), 41, 149, 162
Bratman, Michael, 116
Brennan, Joe, 53
Brennan, Samantha, 168
Brewster, Kingman, 42n1
British idealism, 12. *See also* Anglo-
   idealism
Broad, C. D., 8, 51
Broadie, Sarah, 79
Bronk, Detlev, 114, 115, 116
Brown, Stuart, 27–28
Brown, Wendy, 167
Bryn Mawr College, 94
Buckley, William, 92
Burnham, James, 67
Burnyeat, Myles, 43n4, 103
Bush, George W., 93
Butler, Judith, 95, 165

Calhoun, Cheshire, 164
California Institute of Technology, 81
Callahan, Joan, 168

Calvin College, 17–19, 22
Cambridge Anglicans, 33
Cambridge University, 8, 48, 48–50, 51,
   79, 87, 132, 133, 140
campus shootings, 152
care ethics, 164
Carnap, Rudolf, 66, 73, 75, 133
Carroll, Noël, 169
Cartwright, Nancy, 77
Cassirer, Ernst, 70, 77
Castoriadis, Cornelius, 95
Cavell, Stanley, 153, 160
Change (magazine), 95
Chekola, Mark, 165
Chicago Circle. *See* University of Illinois,
   Chicago
Chicago Psychoanalytic Institute, 74
Child, I., 72
Chisholm, Roderick, 6, 15
Christianity, 18, 25–26, 41, 130, 134, 142,
   142–143, 144
Church, Alonzo, 71–72
civil rights movement, 92
Coburn, Robert, 133
Coffin, William Sloane, 92
cognitive psychology, 141
Cohen, Marshall, 55, 115
Cohen, Ted, 154
Coleman, Jules, 116
College de France, 80
Collingwood, R. G., 19
Collins, Arthur, 53
Columbia University, 51, 51–52, 52, 53,
   87, 100
Committee for Philosophy of the
   Educational Testing Service, 80
computers, 124
conceptual analysis, 11, 12, 21, 124, 133
Consequentialism, 58, 59
consistency, 78
continental philosophy, 120; analytic
   philosophy vs., 11, 90, 99–100,
   117–118, 120; criticisms of, 118;
   feminism and, 162
Cooper, John, 41
Cornell University, 27–29, 110–111, 112,
   130, 132–137, 148
counterfactuals, 11, 19, 57
Cramer, Konrad, 41

Cresswell, Max, 81
Critical Realism, 48, 53, 109
Crocker, David, 93

Daly, Mary, 161–162
Danto, Arthur, 53
Dartmouth University, 152, 160, 161–162
Dauer, Francis, 153
Davidson, Donald, 115, 117, 122, 125
Davis, Angela, 165
Debs, Eugene Victor, 63
deconstruction, 79
Della Roca, Michael, 82
De Man, Paul, 79
demarcation problem, 10
Derrida, Jacques, 79, 98, 100
Descartes, René, 7, 9, 113, 116, 133, 140
determinism, 13
Devlin, Lord, 156
Dewey, John, 2, 40, 64, 66, 89, 92, 95, 100, 125
dialectic, 11
Dickie, George, 77
Diggs, Bill, 130–131, 142
disconfirmation, 10
Dobzhansky, Theodosius, 115
dogmatism, 124, 133, 135, 137, 139
Doney, Willis, 154, 161
Dore, Clem, 5
Dreyfus, Hubert, 12
Du Bois, W. E. B., 166
Duke University, 81

Earle, William, 78
Eaton, Marcia, 77
Eddington, Arthur, 58–59
Edelstein, Ludwig, 113, 114, 115
Educational Testing Service, 80
Edwards, Paul, 32
Einaudi, Mario, 28
Einstein, Albert, 75, 124
Eisenberg, Paul, 154
Elder, J. P., 8
Elliston, Frederick, 159
Encyclopedia of Unified Science, 66
Engels, Friedrich, 160
English, Jane, 159
environmental ethics, 165

epistemology, 6, 109. *See also* meta-epistemology
equality, 123
essentialism, 75
Essler, Wilhelm, 82
ethics, 14, 55, 56, 122, 130, 164. *See also* analytic ethics; applied ethics; metaethics
evil, 129, 130, 131, 132, 135, 143, 145, 146, 147, 167
Ewing, A. C., 51
existentialism, 130
expressivism, 55, 59

Faith and Philosophy (journal), 143
Fanton, Jonathan, 101
Farrell, Daniel, 116
Farrell, Frank, 81
Fassnacht, Robert, 156
FEAST (Society for Feminist Ethics and Social Philosophy), 168
Feferman, Solomon, 80
Feinberg, Joel, 115, 117, 155, 158
Feldman, Fred, 77
feminism, 12, 154, 158, 159, 160, 161–163, 165, 166–167
Feminist Epistemology, Metaphysics, and Science Studies (FEMSS), 168
feminist philosophy, 151, 158, 159, 160, 161–163, 166, 167, 168
feminist separatism, 161, 163
FEMSS (Feminist Epistemology, Metaphysics, and Science Studies), 168
Feyerabend, Paul, 15
Fine, David, 156
Fine, Kit, 81
Firth, Roderick, 6, 154
Fitch, F. B., 69, 70, 71
Flew, Antony, 6
Fogelin, Robert, 79, 81
Foot, Philippa, 132
foreknowledge, 137
form criticism, 144
foundationalism, 6, 11, 14, 15. *See also* anti-foundationalism
Franciscan Institute, 140
Frankena, William, 41, 154, 156
Frankfurt School, 95

Fraser, Nancy, 95, 96, 167
freedom, 146
free will, 121
Frege, Gottlob, 51, 110, 133, 135
Freud, Sigmund, 101, 146
friendship, 99, 100
Frye, Marilyn, 159, 161, 162, 168
Fuchs, Alan, 154
Fulbright Committee, 80
Fulbright scholarship, 48
Fuller, Margaret, 160

Gadamer, Hans-Georg, 97, 98, 100, 120
Garrett, Don, 81
Gass, Bill, 28
Geach, Peter, 51, 76
Gert, Bernie, 152
Gettier, Edmund, 59
Gibbard, Allan, 154
GI Bill, 105
Giddens, Anthony, 95
Gilman, Charlotte Perkins, 160
Ginet, Carl, 113
Glodowski, Shelley, 169
God: conceptions of, 134, 135, 138; and
     evil, 129, 135, 143, 145, 147; existence
     of, 33, 130, 135; reality of, 134
Goldman, Emma, 160
Goldschmidt, Nils, 167
Gomberg, Paul, 154
Goodman, Nelson, 15, 57
Gould, Carol, 159
gray zones, 167
Greenspan, Pat, 81
Gregory of Nyssa, 7
Grewe, Rudolf, 77
Grice, Paul, 125, 132
Griffin, Susan, 161, 165
Grünbaum, Adolf, 74
Guggenheim Fellowship, 74

Habermas, Jürgen, 95, 96, 97, 98, 100,
     120
Hacking, Ian, 77
Hanson, Karen, 2
Hare, R. M., 6, 31, 55
Harris, H. S., 113
Harris, Leonard, 165
Hart, Herbert, 125, 155, 158

Hartman, Geoffrey, 99
Harvard University, 5–8, 10–12, 12, 27,
     52, 69, 153–155
Hausman, Dan, 168, 169
Haverford College, 94–95
Hay, William H., 151
Hegel, G. W. F., 11, 47, 89, 90, 95, 97,
     143
Heidegger, Martin, 12, 93, 120, 125, 167
Heller, Ágnes, 95, 100
Hempel, Carl, 5
Hempel, Peter, 90
Hibben, John Grier, 27
al-Hibri, Azizah, 162
Hick, John, 143
Hilbert, David, 68
Hill, Thomas E., Jr., 154
Hintikka, Jaakko, 133
history of ideas, 109
history of philosophy: analytic philosophy
     and, 15–16, 19, 33, 91, 122, 133, 140;
     attitudes toward, 41–42, 51; and
     medieval philosophy, 138–140; in mid-
     twentieth century, 7, 133; recent
     developments in, 15–16
Hitler, Adolf, 145
Hoagland, Sarah, 164, 165
Hobbes, Thomas, 131
Hobson, Laura, 26
Hofstadter, Albert, 67, 68
Holmes, Oliver Wendell, Jr., 90
Holocaust, 167
Honneth, Axel, 167
honor code, 145
Hook, Sidney, 66, 67, 68
horrors, 132, 135, 143, 145. See also evil
Hull, Clark, 72
human integrity and worth, 143, 145, 146
humanitarian values, 167
Hume, David, 131, 133, 137, 140
Hunter College, CUNY, 37–38, 65
Hunter College High School, 48
Husserl, Edmund, 11, 120
Hutchins, Robert, 27
Hypatia (journal), 160, 162, 164

idealism, 12, 68
incompatibilist freedom, 146
Indiana University Press, 164

Institut International de Philosophie, 79
intensional logic, 72, 74
International Association of Women
    Philosophers, 167
International Congress of Logic,
    Methodology, and Philosophy of
    Science, 79
International Federation of Philosophical
    Sciences, 79
Internet, 43n4, 151
intuitionism, 31, 32

Jaeger, Werner, 7
Jaggar, Alison, 159, 162, 168
James, William, 101, 103, 125, 151
Jeffrey, Dick, 73
Jellema, Harry, 17
Jevons, W. S., 48
Jews and Judaism, 25–27, 42n1, 87, 152,
    167
Jobs in Philosophy/Jobs for Philosophers,
    34, 151
John Dewey Society, 92
John of the Cross, Saint, 29
Johns Hopkins University, 38, 39, 41,
    109–110, 112, 117
Johnson, Alvin, 101
Jonas, Hans, 93
Jubien, Michael, 116
Jung, C. G., 146
justice, 131, 162, 164
justified true belief theory of knowledge,
    59

Kallen, Horace, 101
Kant, Immanuel, 11, 13, 14, 17, 19, 27,
    28, 38, 40, 41, 47, 70, 95, 131, 133,
    140, 143, 145, 166
Kaplan, David, 74
Kerrey, Bob, 93
Kierkegaard, Søren, 90, 130
King, Martin Luther, 36
Köhler, Wolfgang, 112
Korean War, 105
Körner, Stephan, 79
Krebs, Angelika, 167
Kretzmann, Norman, 113
Kripke, Saul, 5, 115, 117, 122, 125, 141
Kuhn, Thomas, 10, 15

Lacey, Nicola, 155
Lauener, Henri, 81, 82
Lawson, Bill, 165
Lazerowitz, Morris, 31, 32
Lear, Jonathan, 116
Leibniz, Gottfried Wilhelm, 70, 133, 140
Leo XIII, Pope, 140
Levi, Isaac, 81
Levi, Primo, 167
Lévinas, Emmanuel, 99, 120
Levison, Arnold, 77
Lewis, C. I., 5, 31, 68, 70, 75
Lewis, David, 6, 57, 122, 141, 148, 154
LGBT issues, 152, 156, 160, 164, 165
Library of Congress, 71
Liebling, A. J., 87
linguistic analysis, 31, 133
Linsky, Leonard, 74
Locke, John, 7, 13, 16, 133, 140
logic, 48, 133. See also intensional logic;
    mathematical logic; modal logic;
    symbolic logic
logical empiricism, 90
logical positivism, 10–12, 12, 13, 15, 66
Lott, Tommy, 165
Lovejoy, Arthur, 66, 109–110
Lowell, A. Lawrence, 27
Lugones, María, 158, 165
Lukes, Steven, 95
Lyons, David, 154

MacCallum, Gerald, 152
MacIntyre, Alasdair, 6
Mackie, J. L., 135
Maddy, Penelope, 81
Maimonides, Moses, 137
Malament, David, 116
Malcolm, Norman, 30, 34, 110, 111, 132,
    133
Mandelbaum, Maurice, 37
Mann, Bill, 39
Mann, Bonnie, 168
Marcus, Ruth Barcan, 151
Margenau, Henry, 70
Martin, Tony, 115, 117
Marx, Karl, 92, 95, 97
Marxism, 64
Massachusetts Institute of Technology
    (MIT), 56, 81

mathematical logic, 122
Maudlin, Tim, 81
McAlister, Linda Lopez, 167
McCarthy, Joseph, 91, 94
McGary, Howard, 165
McKinsey, J. C. C., 68
McTaggart, John, 32, 35
Mead, George Herbert, 95
medieval philosophy, 14, 138–140, 141, 143
Merleau-Ponty, Maurice, 120
meta-epistemology, 6, 11, 14–15
metaethics, 6, 11, 55
metaphilosophy, 60
metaphysics, 6, 14, 32, 56, 66, 75, 133, 134, 141
Mill, John Stuart, 31, 32, 33, 36, 42, 47, 131, 160
Millett, Kate, 161
Mills, Charles, 165
Minas, J. Sayer, 113
Minc, G. E., 79
Mind (journal), 91
mind-body problem, 123
Mississippi Summer Project, 92
modal logic, 5, 68–69, 70, 71–72, 73, 74, 75, 76
modernity, 22
modern philosophy, 13
Mohr, Richard, 164, 165
Montague, William Pepperell, 47
Moody, Ernest, 140
Moody-Adams, Michele, 165
Moore, G. E., 31, 48, 51, 54, 54–55, 58, 122, 125, 133
moral dilemmas, 78
morality, religion and, 26, 27
moral luck, 57, 162–163
moral philosophy, 32–33, 35, 127, 130–131
moral psychology, 121
Moravcsik, Julius, 154
Morgenbesser, Sidney, 53
Morris, Herbert, 155, 158
Mory's, New Haven, Connecticut, 69, 78, 91
Moss, Jessica, 81
Mothersill, Mary, 40, 83
Moulton, John, 160

Murdoch, Iris, 80
Murphy, Arthur, 28, 31
Murray, Nicholas Butler, 100

Nagel, Ernest, 53, 115
Nagel, Thomas, 57, 115, 154, 163
names, 76
Nation (magazine), 92
National Endowment for the Humanities, 80
National Science Foundation, 80
National Women's Studies Association, 162
Nazi Germany, 145
nepotism rule, 56, 74, 78, 149
neuroscience, 123
New Realism, 48, 53, 109
New School for Social Research, 92, 98, 100
New York University, 65–69
Nichols, Mike, 87
Niebuhr, Reinhold, 131
Nielsen, Kai, 162
Nietzsche, Friedrich, 67, 90
Noddings, Nel, 165
Northrup, F. S. C., 70
Northwestern University, 74, 78
Nozick, Robert, 115, 153

Objective Realism, 48, 53
Ockham, William of, 135, 137, 139, 140
Offe, Claus, 95
Ohio State University, 105, 106, 113
old boys' network, 9, 34, 43n6, 77
O'Neill, Onora, 154
ordinary language philosophy, 12–13, 31, 48–49, 66, 122, 133, 134, 138
other minds problem, 50
Otto, Max, 152
Outlaw, Lou, 165
Oxford University, 12, 49, 79, 87, 132, 133, 140, 149

Palade, George, 115
Pap, Arthur, 90
Parfit, Derek, 40, 41
Parsons, Charles, 81, 154
Parsons, Terence (Terry), 75, 77, 81
Patton, Tom, 5

Peirce, Charles Sanders, 40, 90, 95
perception, 109
perspectivalism, 12, 17, 18
Phillips, D. Z., 133–134
Philo, 7
Philosophical Review (journal), 91
philosophical theology, 14, 135, 139, 142, 143
philosophy: changes in profession of, 12, 17, 27, 36, 78, 151–152, 165; criticisms of profession of, 147–149; dogmatism in, 124, 133, 135, 137, 139; employment in, 8, 29, 31, 34, 43n6, 52, 53, 57, 70, 106–107, 107, 108, 151, 152; future of, 56–60, 125–128; historical context of, 15, 20–21, 33, 42, 133; and limits of thought, 13–14; medieval, 14, 138–140, 141, 143; modern, 13; other disciplines in relation to, 14, 147; policing function of, 13–14, 16; positivism and, 11, 13; problems as focus of, 15, 21, 48, 51, 54; professional expansion of, 106–107, 107; publications in, 43n4, 57, 72, 81, 106, 151; religion and, 18–19, 126–128, 130, 132, 134, 135–137, 138–147; research practices in, 33, 72; specialization in, 43n4, 56–57; student interest in, 67, 106; technological impacts on, 151–152; theory in, 59, 60, 141. *See also* analytic philosophy; continental philosophy; history of philosophy
Philosophy and Public Affairs (journal), 55, 122
philosophy of action, 121
philosophy of mind, 141
philosophy of religion, 14, 126, 127, 130, 136, 141, 142–143, 153
philosophy of science, 14, 17, 53, 162
physics, 123, 124, 130
Pierce, Christine, 159
Pike, Nelson, 130, 132, 135, 136–137, 138, 143
Plamenatz, John, 41
Plantinga, Al, 17, 23, 142
Plato, 9, 15, 19, 87, 97, 101, 112, 131, 133, 140, 142, 143
political philosophy, 122–123

Politis, Costas, 53
Popper, Karl, 10, 29
positivism, 11, 13. *See also* logical positivism
possibility, 75
pragmatism, 66, 90, 95, 100
Praxis (journal), 95
Prichard, H. A., 31
Princeton Theological Seminary, 143
Princeton University, 27, 29–31, 35, 37, 81, 119, 144, 154
Prior, Arthur, 74
probability theory, 10
proper names, 76
psychoanalysis, 72, 74, 119, 121, 146
publication, in philosophy, 43n4, 57, 72, 81, 106, 151
Pufendorf, Samuel von, 41
Pugh, John, 165
punishment, 156, 157
purity and defilement calculus, 145
Putnam, Hilary, 78, 102–103, 141

Quakerism, 94
Quine, Willard Van Orman, 5, 13, 15, 41, 69, 75, 76, 81, 93, 115, 116, 122, 125, 133, 153
Quinn, Philip, 39

Radcliffe, Elizabeth, 39, 44n8
Raffman, Diana, 81
Randall, John Herman, 51
rape, 159
Rawls, John (Jack), 6, 21, 30, 34, 35, 40, 57, 122, 125, 131, 148, 153, 154, 154–155, 156, 162
Raz, Joseph, 115
realism, 133–134, 139
redaction criticism, 144
Red Falcons, 63
Reid, Thomas, 7, 17, 21
religion: morality and, 26, 27; personal experiences of, 18, 25–27, 126, 129–130, 135; philosophy and, 18–19, 126–128, 130, 132, 134, 135–137, 138–147
Review of Metaphysics (journal), 93
Rhees, Rush, 133
Rich, Adrienne, 161

Rieff, Philip, 87
Robson, John, 33
Rockefeller Foundation, 72, 79, 80
Rockefeller Institute (later University), 113–117
Roosevelt College, 74
Rorty, Richard (Dick), 40, 42, 87, 89, 91, 93, 95, 96, 97, 100
Roskies, Adina, 81
Roth, Philip, 87
Rothschild, Christine, 156
Ruddick, Sara, 165
rule utilitarianism, 131
Russell, Bertrand, 50, 70, 76, 81, 122, 125, 133
Ryle, Gilbert, 49, 125

Sabine, George, 28
Sachs, David, 41, 133, 137
Sage School of Philosophy. See Cornell University
Salper, Roberta, 36
Sartre, Jean-Paul, 120
Scanlon, Tim, 154
Schaffer, Jerry, 31
Scheffler, Israel, 2
Schmidt, Doro, 167
Schmucker, Josef, 38
Schneewind, Jerry, 78
scholasticism, 139
Schopenhauer, Arthur, 67
science, 10–11. See also neuroscience; philosophy of science; physics
Scotus, Duns, 135, 146
SDS. See Students for a Democratic Society
Searle, John, 79
Seitz, Frederick, 116
Sellars, Wilfrid, 18, 35, 78, 91, 93, 95
sense-datum theory, 30
sense reports, 10
sexism, 148, 153
sexuality, 156. See also LGBT issues
Shalala, Donna, 38
Shapiro, Larry, 169
Sheldon Traveling Fellowship, 8
Shelton, La Verne, 165
Shepere, Dudley, 113
Shoemaker, Sydney, 113, 115

Shumer, Sara, 97
Sidgwick, Henry, 28, 30, 31, 32, 32–33, 35, 37, 38, 40, 41, 42
Simchen, Ori, 81
Simons, Margaret, 159, 164, 168
Singer, Marcus, 152
Sinnott-Armstrong, Walter, 81
skepticism, 13, 133, 139
Skinner, B. F., 13
Skinner, Quentin, 33
Skyrms, Brian, 77
Slote, Michael, 154
Smeenk, Chris, 81
Smiley, Timothy, 132
Smith, James Ward, 31
Smith, John, 35
Smith, John E., 89
Smith, Norman Kemp, 18
Smith, Robin, 39
Smith, Steve, 154
Smith College, 31
Smullyan, Arthur, 72
Soames, Scott, 48, 49, 55
Soares, Joseph A., 42n1
social anthropology, 144
socialism, 63
Society for Analytical Feminism, 162, 168
Society for Feminist Ethics and Social Philosophy (FEAST), 168
Society for Interdisciplinary Feminist Phenomenology, 168
Society for Lesbian and Gay Philosophy (SLGP), 165
Society for Medieval and Renaissance Philosophy, 141
Society for the Study of Women Philosophers, 168
Society for Women in Philosophy (SWIP), 77, 159–160, 162, 165
Society of Christian Philosophers, 142, 142–143
Socrates, 93, 118, 119
Sontag, Susan, 87
Sorabji, Richard, 133
Sosa, Ernest, 81
source criticism, 144
speckled hen problem, 6
Spinoza, Baruch, 7
spirituality, 128

Stace, Walter, 31, 37
Stalin, Joseph, 63
Stalnaker, Robert, 57, 81
Stanford Center for Advance Study in the
  Behavioral Sciences, 79
Stanford University, 39
State University of New York (SUNY) at
  Binghamton, 113
Stein, Ed, 165
Steiner, George, 87
Sterling Hall four, 156
Stevenson, Charles, 6, 70, 77
Stob, Henry, 17–18
Stocker, Michael, 154
Strauss, Leo, 77, 93
Strawson, P. F., 133
Students for a Democratic Society (SDS),
  92
Sullivan, Louis, 74
Superson, Anita, 168
Swinburne, Richard, 131, 143
symbolic logic, 5, 10

Tait, William, 77
Taylor, Charles, 95, 96
teaching and pedagogy, 37, 54, 95, 101,
  137, 148, 152
Teller, Paul, 77
Thalberg, Irving, 77
Tharpe, Lester, 115
theism, 135
theology, 147, 149
Thomas, Laurence, 165, 166
Thomas, Norman, 63
Thomason, Rich, 78
Thomson, James, 56, 83
Thomson, Judith Jarvis, 39, 81, 82–84
Thoreau, Henry David, 27
Tillich, Paul, 80
Tito, Josip, 95
Todes, Sam, 78
Tolstoy, Leo, 19
Toulmin, Stephen, 31
Touraine, Alain, 95
Trebilcot, Joyce, 159
Truth, Sojourner, 160

university/departmental administration,
  36–38, 77, 158

University in Exile, 101
University of California at Irvine, 82
University of California at Los Angeles
  (UCLA), 79, 132, 140, 149
University of Chicago, 32, 40, 41, 73, 77,
  87, 89
University of Illinois, Champaign-Urbana,
  130, 132
University of Illinois, Chicago (Chicago
  Circle), 77, 83
University of Massachusetts-Amherst, 81
University of Michigan, 149
University of Pennsylvania, 94
University of Pittsburgh, 35, 36–37, 41,
  78, 160
University of Wisconsin, 151, 152, 154,
  156, 161, 162, 167, 168–169
Urmson, J. O., 31
U.S. Army, 32, 112
U.S. Health, Education, and Welfare
  Department, 149
utilitarianism, 32, 131

verifiability criterion, 19
verificationism, 133
Vetterling-Braggin, Mary, 159
Vienna Circle, 133
Vietnam War, 35, 55, 78, 92, 94
Vlastos, Gregory, 28, 32, 112
Von Wright, G. H., 51

Wainwright, Bill, 130
Wang, Hao, 115, 117
Wartofsky, Marx, 159
Washington, Booker T., 166
Weber, Max, 22
Weinberg, Julius, 152
Weinstein, Scott, 116
Weiss, Paul, 90, 91, 93
Well, Vivian, 77
Wellmer, Albrecht, 95
Wells, Ida, 160
Westbrook, Robert, 2
Wexler, Jacqueline, 37, 38
Wheelwright, Philip, 67
Whewell, William, 32–33, 33
White, Morton, 154
Whitehead, Alfred North, 7–8, 101, 112,
  125

Whiting, J., 72
Wick, Warner, 32, 41
Wieck, Fred, 97
Wiener Kreis, 133
Wiggins, David, 81
Wikler, Dan, 167
Wild, John, 12
will, 121
Williams, Bernard, 57, 163
Williams, D. C., 6, 7, 8, 12, 13
Williamson, Timothy, 59, 60, 82
Wilson, Margaret, 115
Wisdom, John, 8, 48, 49, 49–50, 53
Wittgenstein, Ludwig, 12, 28, 31, 48–49,
   50, 51, 54, 90, 110–111, 125, 133,
   133–134, 135, 142
Wolf, Susan, 81, 131
Wolff, Bob, 5
Wolfson, Harry, 7
Wollstonecraft, Mary, 160
Wolterstorff, Nick, 143
women: in academia, 69, 77, 78, 84, 91,
   94, 149, 154; discrimination against,
   52, 69, 72, 91, 153, 154; in philosophy,

17, 27, 40, 52, 53, 77, 83, 148–149,
   153, 154, 158–159, 165, 168–169. See
   also feminism; feminist philosophy
women's studies, 36, 78, 161, 162, 164
Women's Studies International Quarterly/
   Forum, 164
Wood, Allen, 145
Woolf, Virginia, 160
World War I, 100
World War II, 70–71, 87

Yale Divinity School, 143
Yale Institute for Human Relations, 72
Yale Psychiatric Institute, 9
Yale University, 8–9, 12, 22, 35, 42n1,
   69–71, 72, 78–79, 81, 82, 89–92, 99,
   117–119
Yolton, John, 32
Young, Iris, 159, 166, 167
Yovel, Yirmiyahu, 100

Zack, Naomi, 165
Ziff, Paul, 12, 77

ABOUT THE CONTRIBUTORS

Steven M. Cahn (b. 1942) is professor of philosophy at the Graduate Center of the City University of New York.

Nicholas Wolterstorff (b. 1932) is Noah Porter Emeritus Professor of Philosophical Theology at Yale University. He served as president of the Central Division of the American Philosophical Association in 1991–1992.

J. B. Schneewind (b. 1930) is professor emeritus of philosophy at Johns Hopkins University. He served as president of the Eastern Division of the American Philosophical Association in 1995–1996 and chair of the Board of Officers of the American Philosophical Association from 1999 to 2002.

Judith Jarvis Thomson (b. 1929) is professor emerita of philosophy at Massachusetts Institute of Technology. She served as president of the Eastern Division of the American Philosophical Association in 1992–1993 and chair of the Board of Officers of the American Philosophical Association from 2002 to 2005.

Ruth Barcan Marcus (1921–2012) was professor emerita of philosophy at Yale University. She served as president of the Central (then Western) Division of the American Philosophical Association in 1975–1976 and chair of the Board of Officers of the American Philosophical Association from 1977 to 1983.

Richard J. Bernstein (b. 1932) is Vera List Professor of Philosophy at The New School for Social Research. He served as president of the Eastern Division of the American Philosophical Association in 1988–1989.

Harry Frankfurt (b. 1929) is professor emeritus in the Department of Philosophy at Princeton University. He served as president of the Eastern Division of the American Philosophical Association in 1990–1991.

Marilyn McCord Adams (b. 1943) is distinguished research professor in the Department of Philosophy at the University of North Carolina at Chapel Hill. She served as president of the Society for Medieval and Renaissance Philosophy from 1980 to 1982. She is also an Episcopal priest and Canon Emeritus at Christ Church Cathedral, Oxford.

Claudia Card (b. 1940) is Emma Goldman Professor of Philosophy at the University of Wisconsin–Madison. She served as president of the Central Division of the American Philosophical Association in 2010–2011.